Criminality and Its Treatment: The Patuxent Experience

CRIMINALITY AND ITS TREATMENT: THE PATUXENT EXPERIENCE

FRANCIS L. CARNEY, Ph.D.

Psychology Services Chief,
Patuxent Institution
and
Clinical Assistant Professor of Psychiatry,
University of Maryland School of Medicine

ROBERT E. KRIEGER PUBLISHING COMPANY

MALABAR, FLORIDA
1989

Original Edition 1989

Printed and Published by
ROBERT E. KRIEGER PUBLISHING CO., INC.
KRIEGER DRIVE
MALABAR, FLORIDA 32950

Library of Congress Cataloging-in-Publication Data

Carney, Francis L.
    Criminality and its treatment : Patuxent experience / by Francis
L. Carney.
      p. cm.
    Bibliography: p.
    Incluces index.
    ISBN 0-89464-348-7 (alk. paper)
    1. Patuxent Institution (Md.) 2. Rehabilitation of criminals-
-Maryland--Jessup. 3. Criminal psychology. 4. Social work with
delinquents and criminals--Maryland--Jessup. 5. Drug abuse-
-Treatment--Maryland--Jessup. 6. Pedophilia--Treatment--Maryland-
-Jessup. I. Title.
HV9306.J472P383 1989
364.3'01'9--dc19   88-8444
                                        CIP

10   9   8   7   6   5   4   3   2

Preface

This book comes from my some thirty years experience in the field of criminal justice, most of it as a psychologist, but including in my early career several years' experience as a probation officer for a juvenile court. I have also worked on the forensic ward of a large state psychiatric hospital, in mental health clinics, and with a special offenders clinic associated with a medical school. However, the larger part of my professional career has been spent at the Patuxent Institution in Maryland, which is a unique combination of a maximum security prison and a psychiatric hospital; it is from this institution that the majority of my case material is drawn, and it was here that most of my ideas about criminals and the treatment of criminals were formed. Patuxent is not a conventional prison, there has always been some room for innovative psychiatric practice, but Patuxent also exemplifies many of the problems in that uneasy partnership between psychiatry and the law, and that even more uneasy relationship between corrections and public policy. No discussion of the treatment of criminality can ignore its political aspects.

It is axiomatic that there are no easy answers to the problems of crime and criminality, but even so a tendency to take extreme positions exists: some advocate more extreme punishments opposed to those who advocate more and better treatment; there is the focus on the suffering of the victim or the focus on the environmental conditions which produced the criminal; and there is the emphasis on the welfare of society as opposed to the welfare of the individual. These are generally presented as antagonistic positions which admit no middle ground, a dichotomy which might inevitably be characterized as the difference between the individual's responsibility to society and society's responsibility to the individual. I question that these antagonistic positions *have* to exist. In well run corrections departments new officers are taught that the act of imprisonment, the deprivation of liberty, is the punishment, and added punishments within the prison are unnecessary. That this philosophy rarely becomes practice is tragic, for what makes the difference in corrections is not how much time a man spends in prison but what happens to him while he's there. To some extent the arguments over short versus long sentences, determinate as opposed to indeterminate sentences, are specious. *Any* deprivation of liberty is punishing, and when sentence is imposed, the state is exercising its right to punish transgressors against its laws and meeting its obligations to society as a whole. I doubt that anyone would deny the state that right. But then to go on and assume that the punishment is also curative is folly, for experience has taught that it is only curative for some, and that those who are destined for careers in crime, if affected at all by the prison experience, are affected in a negative way. If the state really means to protect society, it cannot simply lock the criminal away for X-number of years and forget about him. Within the secure environment, while keeping dangerous people away from innocent citizens, the state has the obligation to treat so as to prevent future crimes. Probably few people would disagree with that either, but "treatment" would have a lot of definitions.

In the following pages I intend to explore the dynamics of criminality and their implications for treatment and psychotherapy, and while much of the focus will be on treatment in prisons, it should be noted that most criminals, in the course of their careers, receive some outpatient care, generally as a condition of probation or parole. It should also be noted that psychotherapy, as one possible method, need not necessarily be the treatment of choice; indeed, the dynamics of criminality suggest that millieu and supportive therapies and directive counseling may often be more effective. And while criminality is the subject of this book, its inevitable emphasis is on those severe personality disorders which are as challenging and frustrating in hospital and private practice as they are in prison.

The views I express throughout this book are entirely those of the author. Specifically, they do not necessarily represent the views, positions, or policies of Patuxent Institution, the Maryland State Department of Public Safety and Correctional Services, or of any other agency, official, or employee of the state of Maryland.

The names of all patients are fictitious. Case history material has been altered so as to preserve dynamics while further disguising the identity of the individual.

Contents

1
Prisoners and Patients

When the Patuxent Institution opened its doors in 1955, the director and two of the three associate directors were psychiatrists, there was a small professional staff of psychologists and social workers, and the residents were called "patients." In those days Patuxent was the darling of psychiatry, it soon broke away from corrections to become an independent state agency which answered directly to the governor through an organization known as the Board of Patuxent Institution, and this board was dominated by the mental health establishment. The influence of corrections was hardly felt at all. Then times changed, the institution became an agency under the Department of Public Safety and Correctional Services, two of the administrative psychiatric positions were lost, the psychiatric community in general was excluded from participation in planning and programing, and the residents of Patuxent today are called "inmates." Thus, language tends to define existing conditions.

The above is greatly oversimplified, for the Patuxent of the 1950s *could not* exist in the 1980s. Times do change, which means that the will of the public changes, attitudes and opinions change, and corrections, in whatever guise, is the servant, if not the slave, of politics. But "patient" or "inmate," the dynamics of behavior are unchanged; the change is in our response to them.

The history of Patuxent Institution tends to illustrate many of the problems encountered when the mental health professions interface

1

with corrections. There have really been "two" Patuxent Institutions because of changing philosophies and laws, and the two institutions combine to form one "laboratory."

PATUXENT: HOW IT BEGAN AND HOW IT CHANGED

The original Patuxent was created after a number of research reports were submitted to the Maryland Legislature in 1949 and 1950, particularly the report of the Committee to Study Medico-Legal Psychiatry. The committee was formed to address the problem of "psychopathic personalities" and what to do with them in the criminal justice system. It was chaired by Jerome Robinson, a legal scholar, and was assisted by such mental health notables as John C. Whitehorn, Manfred Guttmacher, and Robert M. Lindner. The final report to the legislature was titled *An Indeterminate Sentence Law for Defective Delinquents* (Reiblich & Hubbard, 1950), in which it was stated:

> The primary purpose of such legislation is to protect society from this segment of the criminal population who will probably again commit crimes if released on the expiration of a fixed sentence; and thus they should be detained and specifically treated unless and until cured. A secondary purpose is more effectively and humanely to handle them, which aids in the cure, where possible. (p. 1)

To the above, the psychiatric consultants added, "Many of these individuals cannot be cured by any present treatment techniques" (p. 27).

The law which grew out of this report was Article 31B of the Public General Laws of Maryland, and it was called the Defective Delinquency Law. A defective delinquent was defined as any individual currently serving a sentence in Maryland who was (1) emotionally unbalanced and/or mentally deficient, who (2) demonstrated a history of persistent, aggravated antisocial behavior, and who (3) was deemed to be a danger to society. Such defective delinquents were to be confined at Patuxent Institution and treated until they were no longer dangerous to society, or forever. The intent of the law, clearly, was confinement in a humane environment. Few experts expected there would be many successful cures. (For a more complete description see F. L. Carney, 1974; Wilner, 1983.)

The institution itself was to be neither a prison nor a mental hospital but some curious combination of both. In design, it looks like a maximum security prison with the usual complement of bars, grills, and gates. It differs from most maximum security prisons in that it was built to house only six hundred inmates, and it's so designed that one guard is rarely responsible for more than forty-four inmates. This has implication for the safety needs of the inmates, so that even during the most turbulent period in Patuxent's history few inmates or staff were seriously hurt. In more than thirty years, Patuxent has had only one murder and only five suicides, and documented incidents of rape are extremely rare. The institution's design facilitates good mental hygiene practice, but the ultimate responsibility for the creation of a therapeutic milieu rests with the staff of psychiatrists, psychologists, and social workers who are the managers of all programs within the institution. However, this doesn't relegate correctional officers to the status of "poor cousins," for none of the programs would be possible without the maintenance of the secure environment and the active cooperation of the officers.

One of the most important features of Article 31B was the creation of the Institutional Board of Review, to be composed of the director, the three associate directors, and four members from the community: a sociologist, a professor of constitutional law, and two practicing attorneys. The board was mandated to see every committed inmate and to review his progress at least once per calendar year, and the board was given the authority to approve inmates for conditional release status. This "status" takes the following forms: *leaves* to the community, which allow the inmate to be away from the institution for as many as five days a month; *work release*, during which period the inmate lives in the institution (or Patuxent's Re-Entry Facility in Baltimore) but works in the community; *school release*, which permits the man to go to school in the community while he continues to live in the institution (or the Re-Entry Facility); and *parole*, which permits the man to live and work in the community while remaining under the supervision of Patuxent's professional staff. Thus, Patuxent Institution was empowered to be its own paroling authority, and as a consequence outpatient services became as much a part of treatment as inpatient services. Still, the intent of the law was confinement, and the framers of the law probably never guessed that the outpatient services would become as important as they did.

It was probably naive to expect that mental health professionals would settle for being caretakers in a warehouse for humans, and, as we shall see, there were also forces at work which would cause a shift in emphasis from warehousing to treatment, rehabilitation, and release. In a small institution like Patuxent it was possible to study closely the behavior and psychology of the defective delinquents, who for the most part really were psychopathic personalities, and treatment strategies and techniques were developed. (See, for example, Boslow & Kohlmeyer, 1963; Boslow, Rosenthal, Kandel, & Manne, 1961.) As a result, the board started to approve men for status in ever increasing numbers, and contrary to all expectations, the recidivism rates weren't bad, though they were subject to contradictory interpretations. Steadman (1977), for example, severely criticized Patuxent's in-house studies, citing methodological errors and statistical manipulation, while his own study indicated that Patuxent's inmates did no better on parole than men from conventional prisons. Hodges (1971), on the other hand, who defined recidivism as conviction for a new felony, indicated that Patuxent's recidivism rate was 20%, a rate achieved after treating defective delinquents who were by definition chronic recidivists. But whatever the interpretation, even if Patuxent wasn't living up to expectations, it certainly wasn't failing.

Patuxent accepted its first inmates in 1955, and the next twenty-two years were marked with controversy. Judge Alan M. Wilner (1983), who has been involved with Patuxent from the very beginning 'as both a judge and a legislator, remembers events in this way:

At first the challenges were mostly legal in nature. The constitutionality of the whole concept of locking up people for an indeterminate period was attacked over and over again. The validity of each of the statutory and operational procedures was attacked over and over again. The determinations respecting the individual inmates committed to Patuxent were attacked by the inmates over and over again. Most of the people committed [to Patuxent] resorted to court as often as possible in order initially to block their commitment and thereafter to be judicially released.

From 1955 to 1976 probably no two consecutive months passed when some feature of the enabling statute or some feature of the operation of Patuxent was not under attack in some court. The staff probably spent as much time defending the institution and institutional decisions as they did in treating the inmates. [And] eventually the attacks became more policy-oriented. Initially, advocacy groups and civil libertarians but gradually a broader spectrum of people began to challenge the *wisdom* of Patuxent as well as its legality. . . .

What happened, was this. In order to defend against the legal attacks centered on the ability to incarcerate someone until a group of doctors certified that he was safe to be released, Patuxent had to stress the concomitant psychotherapeutic program. The . . . Court, though sustaining the facial constitutionality of the law, made clear that it would not permit Patuxent to become "a mere device for

warehousing the obnoxious and antisocial elements of society."
(pp. 6–7)

Starting in the early '70s, more and more pressure was put on the legislature by a wide variety of citizens' groups to abolish Patuxent, and the institution's cause wasn't helped at all by a series of disturbances within its walls. Finally, the governor ordered a study of Patuxent. Judge Wilner continues:

> In fact, two studies were done. The one promised by the Governor was contracted out by the Department of Public Safety and Correctional Services to a Massachusetts consultant known as Contract Research Corporation. The other, which in its inception had nothing to do with Patuxent, was conducted by a gubernatorial commission consisting of a broad spectrum of judges, prosecutors, defense counsel, penologists, and psychiatrists, which I was privileged to chair. . . .
> Our Commission reaffirmed the fact that there were, within the larger group of criminals, a smaller group who, though legally sane, nevertheless by reason of some intellectual or emotional deficiency, are lacking in self-control. These people, we found, have a persistent tendency to criminal behavior and are not usually influenced by conventional penological or reformative measures. We concluded that such people could not be effectively dealt with either by the correctional or the mental health systems alone. Neither was capable, or could practically be made capable, of dealing with this group of people. . . .
> By a process of elimination almost, we began to appreciate the value of a place like Patuxent where in one specialized institution both aspects of security and treatment could be merged. We also concluded, however, that the wrong people were being committed to Patuxent: People who the institution could not help; people who did not want to be helped; people who resisted commitment because of the compulsive requirement to accept unwanted treatment enforced by the indeterminate sentence. The difficulty was not so much the Patuxent concept or even the Patuxent program. The problem was in the entrance requirements and the indeterminate sentence. (pp. 9–11)

The report from the out-of-state consultants (Contract Research Corporation [CRC], 1977) reached pretty much the same conclusions, though these consultants, in general, were less kindly disposed toward the institution than the gubernatorial commission. However, CRC was quite impressed by the Institutional Board of Review and the outpatient services, it generally approved of treatment for prisoners, and it recommended to the legislature that the Defective Delinquency Law be repealed but that Patuxent Institution be retained as a specialized treatment facility. The legislature followed the recommendations and created a "new" Patuxent, which came into existence on July 1, 1977.

The new Article 31B defined a class of inmates who would be called "Eligible Persons." They were defined as persons who (1) had at least three years remaining on a criminal sentence, who (2) were emotionally unbalanced and/or mentally deficient, who (3) were likely to respond favorably to Patuxent's programs, and who (4) could be better rehabilitated at Patuxent than by other incarceration. The institution continued to be its own paroling authority, and both inpatient and outpatient services remained essentially unchanged. However, there was no longer an indeterminate sentence, and inmates had to volunteer for treatment.

When the new law went into effect there was one immediate consequence: all of the inmates serving an indeterminate sentence had their original determinate sentence reimposed, and as a result thirty-three inmates whose sentences had expired were set free. In the next seven years twenty-three of them became recidivists: they were arrested for fifty-eight new crimes ranging from narcotics violations to rape and murder, and they served (or are still serving) new sentences ranging from a few months in jail to life in prison. Of the eight sex offenders in the group, six committed new sex offenses. So the Defective Delinquency Law did do what it was intended to do, prevent more crimes, but it did so at the expense of the ten men who did not commit new crimes. There is ever this question when we treat criminality: Where *do* we draw the line between a man's right to be free and society's right to be safe?

The new Article 31B redefined Patuxent's population. To be a defective delinquent meant to be deemed virtually untreatable, and defective delinquents fought against therapy and had no motivation to change. The eligible person, on the other hand, has to volunteer for treatment in the first place and has to be deemed treatable in the second place. But predicting treatability is hardly an exact science, and Patuxent is popular with prisoners for reasons which have nothing to do with "motivation for change." Patuxent is first of all a safe prison, even safer now than it was in the past because Patuxent doesn't have to keep violent inmates and it doesn't. Second, since Patuxent is its own paroling authority and need pay no attention to "time served" before granting status—as the Parole Commission must—many prisoners with long sentences apply to

Patuxent only for the purpose of "beating" their time. Lifers particularly saw Patuxent as a quick way out. That wasn't the fact, but in 1983, as a result of pressure from citizens' groups who were concerned that lifers were being paroled too soon, Article 31B was emended so that the Board of Review lost its power to parole men who were serving a life sentence. Now, in the case of lifers, the board can only recommend parole to the governor, who makes the final decision.

Treatment practices under the new law differ little from treatment practices under the old law. An attempt is made to provide a therapeutic milieu in which everything—education, vocational shops, discipline, institutional job assignments, etc.—is geared toward the treatment of the individual. Treatment also takes the form of reward and punishment through promotion-demotion in a graded tier system, and, of course, every man is also in group and/or individual psychotherapy; and all of Patuxent's services are still available to the man when he returns to the community. There is a continuity of treatment from admission to eventual discharge.

Other aspects of the program need not concern us here. It is only important to note that Patuxent is essentially a prison designed and managed by mental health specialists, and that in its history its "patients" have been deemed to be the most untreatable and the most treatable of criminals. However, experientially, Patuxent has never been free from the influence—even the direction—of traditional correctional practice; and, dynamically if not behaviorally, there is probably little distinction between the two patient populations. In a sense, for the last thirty years Patuxent has been a laboratory in which old and new ideas have clashed: it is an institution which is a self-contained mini-correctional system which includes aspects of classification-evaluation, correctional practice, prison administration, psychotherapy and rehabilitation, and after care and parole; and it is a psychiatric-correctional entity which is forced to relate to the courts, political departments, and the public. It was and still is a unique experiment in corrections and psychiatry.

TWO (?) PRISONER-PATIENT POPULATIONS

The two laws which governed Patuxent Institution defined two apparently different inmate populations, but how different are they? In 1973 Patuxent delivered to the legislature *A Progress Report* (Patuxent Institution, 1973) which discussed the characteristics of 976 men who were committed as defective delinquents (DDs) between 1955 and 1972. The institution's *Annual Report* for 1983 summarized the characteris-

TABLE 1   Characteristics of Defective Delinquents and Eligible Persons

	Defective Delinquents N = 976	Eligible Persons N = 523
Age at Admission	24.6	24.5
IQ (WAIS)	91.9	90.7
Mean Sentence (yrs.)°	7.8	29.4
Crimes of Murder, Rape, Assault or Robbery	56%	94%
No. Prior Convictions	4.9	0.852°°
Race: White	60%	42%
Non-White	40%	58%

°Life sentences not included. There were 94 men serving life sentences in 1983. Figures for 1972 not available.
°°This figure is not from the *Annual Report* and was calculated later.

tics of the 523 eligible persons (EPs) who were currently in treatment. A comparison of these two populations is found in Table 1.

It is apparent that there is little difference between the two populations with respect to age at admission and intelligence, but after that differences are significant. First, the racial balance has shifted dramatically, a trend that has been going on for thirty years, until now the racial mixture at Patuxent more nearly approximates that of Maryland's prison population, about 25% white and 75% nonwhite. It's difficult to explain these figures, except to note that under the Defective Delinquency Law all referrals to Patuxent were court referrals, and courts referred more whites than blacks. Under the new law, referrals come from a variety of sources, including the prisoners themselves.

Second, to consider seriousness of crime and number of prior convictions as related phenomena: by definition defective delinquents had to be chronic recidivists, and their dangerousness was often related more to their repetitive criminal behavior than to any specific crime. Eligible persons, on the other hand, tend to be selected because they *don't* have a long prior record, and their current conviction for a violent crime may be ego-dystonic.

Third, with regard to sentence, judges weren't too concerned about imposing long sentences when they assumed there would be an eventual commitment for an indeterminate time; and additionally, they were more likely to refer to Patuxent the chronic, petty offender than the major criminal. Also, the times have changed, and courts now impose longer sentences in any event.

TABLE 2 DSM-III Diagnosis of Eligible Persons (N = 542)

	Frequency	Percent
Antisocial Personality	254	46.9
Atypical Mixed Personality	83	15.3
Dependent Personality	44	8.1
Avoidant Personality	22	4.1
Borderline Personality	19	3.5
Passive Aggressive Personality	15	2.8
Intermittent Explosive Disorder	15	2.8
Isolated Explosive Disorder	7	1.3
All Others	67	12.2
Personality Disorder	480	88.5
Disorder of Impulse Control	22	4.1
Conduct Disorders	13	2.3
Psychotic Disorders	11	2.1
Sexual Disorders	6	1.2
All Others	10	1.8

Under the Defective Delinquency Law the Patuxent staff did not make a formal diagnosis of inmates. Because the definition of a defective delinquent anticipates the later criteria in DSM-III for Antisocial Personality Disorder, I think it fair to assume the most DDs were antisocial personalities. Eligible persons are examined, and the primary diagnosis of 542 EPs (in 1984) is presented in Table 2.

Considering that we're dealing with a criminal population, it's not too surprising that most EPs find their diagnosis among the personality disorders (88.5%) and that of these 46.9% are antisocial personalities. (The psychotic disorders are not well represented because Patuxent isn't geared to work with them.) Perhaps most interesting is that very few EPs (8.2%) are diagnosed neurotic, conduct, adjustment, or impulse disorders; i.e., essentially noncriminals who commit an isolated criminal act, for it would be people like this who would probably be considered to be the most treatable of criminals.

Having described the two populations along demographic and diagnostic lines, what are they really like? An early description of Patuxent (Boslow, Rosenthall, & Gliedman, 1958), written when Patuxent was just three years old and only 386 beds large, is illuminating. This first administration of Patuxent conceived of the defective delinquent as follows:

He is basically amoral, shares minimal social values with others, and is flagrantly hedonistic and opportunistic. His crimes are of impulse, sometimes of a compulsive, neurotic nature, and usually involve inadequate planning at best. The paid killer, the racketeer, or the skilled safe-cracker may be noted as examples of the kind of criminal who remains outside the compass of psychiatric jurisdiction . . . whereas examples of defective delinquents include some organic and congenital mental defectives, epileptics, sex offenders, drug addicts, compulsively neurotic criminals such as fire-setters and kleptomaniacs, and some severely amoral people who cannot be assimilated to a usual prison routine. . . . Underlying the principle of the indeterminate sentence is a view of the criminal . . . as someone who is at the mercy of his own needs and impulses. (pp. 7–8)

That was the initial conception of a defective delinquent, but attitudes soon began to change. The *Progress Report* of 1973, for example, stated that between 1955 and 1972 the average length of sentence increased from 4.5 years to 10 years, and convictions for violent crimes from 41% to 71%. The definition of a defective delinquent now seemed to include criminals who were not necessarily "compulsively neurotic" or "severely amoral." It was an evolution which was probably a reaction to two major influences: (1) there probably just weren't enough narrowly-defined defective delinquents to fill the institution after it expanded to 600 beds; and (2) when treatment and release became the goal rather than confinement, both the courts and the staff became interested in committing "good" treatment prospects. I can illustrate the latter point with the case of one young man who came to Patuxent with three consecutive life sentences, who in the 1960s would not have become a defective delinquent because he was already for all intents and purposes confined forever, but in the 1970s the staff felt that he could be and should be treated so that he could one day return to society, and the court agreed. Another example is that of a young man who was serving a twenty-five year sentence for his first and only offense, who was not legally a defective delinquent because he didn't have a history of persistent, aggravated antisocial behavior, but he volunteered for commitment and treatment, the staff wanted to treat him, and the court committed him. But even the original group of defective delinquents wasn't as "untreatable" as the law and psychiatry predicted. Boslow et al. (1958) write:

Not all persons committed as defective delinquents are bitter and fearful. There are a few who realize in an ill-defined way that they need help because their behaviour is repetitive and self-destructive, and they may welcome the haven of externally imposed restrictions in a relatively benign atmosphere. Some may actually favour commitment because their difficulties outside have mounted beyond their capacity to cope with them. Some are malingerers who may be serving long sentences and who see in the commitment procedure an opportunity to pull strings and manipulate others so that they can be released long before the expiration of their sentence. (p. 9)

Making virtually no change, the above paragraph describes Patuxent's current population of eligible persons, the so-called "most treatable" of criminals. For in actual fact, the *best* treatment risks, the *best* potential patients among the prisoners, are those who have led noncriminal and relatively productive lives up to the moment of their crime, those for whom criminal behavior is ego-dystonic, who may be overwhelmed by guilt and anxiety, and who are acutely uncomfortable in the prison environment. There just aren't many people like that in the prison system.

Generally, the *average* DD and the *average* EP are probably more alike than different. It's only when we get away from the *average* that we see the difference between the two populations: the extreme DD was in fact severely amoral and unresponsive to any treatment intervention, and the extreme EP is psychodynamically noncriminal though he committed a criminal act.

The consultants who studied Patuxent concluded that the Defective Delinquency Law failed in its application, that because dangerousness cannot be reliably predicted too many nondangerous men were committed as defective delinquents, and the consultants also felt that many courts used the law to confine petty trouble-makers for long periods of time. I think those conclusions are correct. I believe that under the DD Law Patuxent did not treat only the most untreatable; and under the EP Law Patuxent is not treating only the most treatable. It is better, I believe, to consider the two populations as one population, a population of criminals.

PSYCHIATRIC CHARACTERISTICS OF PRISONERS

The magnitude of the prisoner problem is perhaps indicated by the following:

The number of prisoners under the jurisdiction of Federal and State correctional authorities at yearend 1986 reached a record 546,659. The States and the District of Columbia added 39,203 prisoners; the Federal system, 4,185. The increase for 1986 brings total growth in the prison population since 1980 to nearly 217,000 inmates—an increase of about 66% in the 6-year period. (Bureau of Justice Statistics [BJS], 1987a, p. 1)

On the basis of other information (Greenfeld, 1985) it's not unreasonable to assume that about 61% of those admitted to prison in any given year are recidivists (i.e., they had previously been incarcerated as a juvenile, adult, or both); and that nearly 60% of those admitted to prison for the first time had prior convictions that resulted in probation. It follows, therefore, that the penitentiary prisoner who has *no* prior history of law violations is a very rare bird indeed.

It should also be noted that since 1981 the growth rate for female prisoners has been greater than the rate for males, but even so, women still account for less than 5% of the nation's prisoners (BJS, 1987a). Women prisoners haven't received as much study as males, and until recently the inmate population at Patuxent was exclusively male, so my discussion of criminal behavior is focused on males. However, I have no reason to believe that my comments on criminality should not include females. At least two studies (Guze, 1976; Miller, 1984) indicate that female prisoners are not too unlike their male counterparts.

Generally, prison populations are studied along demographic rather than diagnostic lines, the usual results indicating that young, ethnic-minority, urban males are more likely to be arrested and incarcerated than anyone else (Federal Bureau of Investigation [FBI], 1985). When diagnostic studies are made, they indicate that there is a distinct difference between those who are arrested and jailed as opposed to those who finally go to prison. That is, however inadequate our "insanity" laws may be, they do tend to screen out the seriously mentally ill from the rest of the prison population. Coid (1984), for example, evaluated eleven major studies of prisoners conducted in the United States and Great Britain between 1918 and 1980, and taking into account methodological differences and changes in nomenclature, he found that psychotic disorders occurred in less than 2% of the prison populations. This changes radically when we look at pre-sentence prisoners. In one typical urban jail Guy, Platt, and Zwerling (1985) found that of ninety-six inmates diagnosed, 11.5% were schizophrenic and another 4.2% suffered from a major affective disorder; and in this population only 9.0% were diagnosed as having a personality disorder, and 25% were given *no diag-*

nosis. That last is particularly significant and is related to problems found in jails rather than prisons, especially the incidence of suicide (see Chapter 5).

Another indication that jail inmates are diagnostically different from prison inmates is offered by Protter and Travin (1982). They report on 270 consecutive pre-sentence evaluations in a court psychiatric clinic in the Bronx, New York. Their subjects were 84% male and 16% female; 77% were age range sixteen through thirty; and they were 42% black, 40% Hispanic, and 18% white. Diagnostically, 57% had a psychotic history and 11% were currently schizophrenic; and 32% were diagnosed as having some personality disorder, of whom only 5% were antisocial personalities.

As we leave the jail and enter the prison, not only does the incidence of psychosis decrease, the incidence of personality disorder increases. A major diagnostic study of prisoners was made by Guze (1976) whose subjects were 223 male felons from the Missouri prison system; they were 73% white and 27% nonwhite, and their mean age was twenty-seven to twenty-eight. His subjects were originally diagnosed in 1959, and there was a rediagnosis eight to nine years later when many of them were on parole. There was a statistically reliable agreement between original and follow-up diagnosis, except that sociopathy was over-diagnosed originally, 78% as opposed to 60% on follow-up. Ninety percent of the subjects received some psychiatric diagnosis, of which roughly 85% were among the personality disorders. Only 1% were diagnosed schizophrenic.

A study of referrals made to Patuxent Institution is suggestive though perhaps the results can't be confidently generalized to prison populations as a whole. When a man is examined at Patuxent, he is given a complete diagnostic work-up, which includes physical and psychiatric examinations, psychological testing, and social work evaluation. He is studied and observed for four to six months, and then he appears before a panel of mental health professionals where he is interviewed and examined again. The decision of the panel is whether or not to admit him to Patuxent, but the panel also arrives at a DSM-III diagnosis. Between July 1, 1984 and June 30, 1986 there were 873 men evaluated by Patuxent's staff, of whom 846 received a final diagnosis. The characteristics of these men are presented in Table 3. For comparison purposes, also included in Table 3 are the characteristics of 11,751 men who were prisoners in Maryland's Division of Correction (DOC) institutions on April 30, 1986.

The most striking difference between these two populations is the average length of sentence, which is 20.48 years at Patuxent and 9.65

TABLE 3   Characteristics of Two Prison Populations

	Patuxent Institution	Division of Correction
Number	873	11,751
Non-White	60.50%	73.07%
White	39.50%	26.93%
Average Age (yrs.)	26.45	30.10
Average Sentence (yrs., excluding Life sentence)	20.48	9.65
Life Sentence: No.	73	826
Percent	8.36%	7.02%

years in the DOC. In part, this is because Patuxent cannot (by law) accept men who are serving sentences of less than 3 years, and in the DOC 21.42% of the inmates are serving less than 3 years. Also, it is the men with the longest sentences who tend to volunteer for Patuxent.

Patuxent's inmates also tend to be younger (26.45 years) than the inmates in the DOC (30.10 years). This may be explained by the fact that Patuxent calculates "age at admission" while the DOC calculates "current age." Thus, in the DOC population we have all lumped together men who have just been incarcerated along with men who have already served a significant portion of their sentence.

I have no explanation for the difference in racial composition.

Because these differences do exist, the findings with respect to diagnoses cannot be generalized to Maryland's prison population as a whole, much less to prison populations outside of Maryland. The sample is skewed in the direction of men who are serving the longest sentences and, by implication, have committed the most serious crimes.

Table 4 presents a summary of the primary DSM-III diagnosis of the 846 men who were fully evaluated at Patuxent, whether or not they were eventually accepted for treatment. Not surprising, the personality disorders predominate (87.71%), and the 2.06% psychotic disorders is in keeping with other studies. It is perhaps also significant that there was no diagnosis found in only one case (0.12%).

In Table 5 the incidence of specific personality disorders is presented. Antisocial Personality Disorder is by far (50.12%) the most frequent diagnosis. Next in frequency is Atypical Mixed Personality Disorder (14.54%), which usually includes "with antisocial features." The other personality disorders appear in pure form infrequently, which may re-

TABLE 4 Primary Diagnosis of 846 Prisoners

Diagnosis	Frequency	Percent
No Diagnosis	1	.12
All Psychotic Disorders	22	2.60
All Personality Disorders	742	87.71
Sexual Disorders	20	2.36
Alcohol Dependence	4	.47
Drug Dependence	3	.36
Adjustment Disorders	5	.59
Organic Personality	1	.12
Undersocialized Aggressive	10	1.18
Socialized Aggressive	9	1.06
Explosive Disorders	27	3.19
Developmental Disorders	2	.24

flect DSM-III's emphasis on behavior as opposed to dynamics. (This will be discussed in Chapter 3.)

To complete the diagnostic picture, Table 6 presents a summary of secondary diagnoses of substance abuse. Of these 846 men, 689 (81.44%) received at least one such secondary diagnosis, 342 men (40.42%) received two secondary diagnoses, and 78 men (9.21%) received three secondary diagnoses. Alcohol (abuse or dependence) played a role in the criminal histories of 37.71% of the men, and 72.58% abused or were addicted to some narcotic or combination of

TABLE 5 Primary Diagnosis of Personality Disorder

Diagnosis	Frequency	Percent
Antisocial	424	50.12
Atypical Mixed	123	14.54
Dependent	58	6.86
Borderline	32	3.78
Avoidant	23	2.72
Passive Aggressive	19	2.25
Schizoid	18	2.13
Schizotypal	17	2.01
Paranoid	14	1.65
Narcissistic	10	1.18
Compulsive	2	.24
Histrionic	2	.24

TABLE 6   Secondary Diagnosis of Substance Abuse or Dependence N = 846

Diagnosis	Frequency	Percent
No Diagnosis	157	18.56
Alcohol	319	37.71
Any Drug	614	72.58
PCP	202	23.99
Cannabis	130	15.34
Mixed opiod & non-opiod	95	11.23
Mixed non-opiod	78	9.22
Opiod	47	5.56
Cocaine	16	1.89
Other	6	.71

narcotics. These findings with respect to substance abuse are consistent with national surveys. (See Chapter 6.)

On the whole, it seems fair to say that the criminal justice system does an adequate—not perfect—job of screening out of prison those who don't need to be there, namely, those who are seriously mentally ill and those who have no psychiatric disorder. What's left, accounting for roughly 85% of the prison population, are the personality disorders, particularly the antisocial personality. The question is whether or not these prisoners should ever become patients, or is imprisonment alone treatment enough? And as a "treatment," does it work?

A study (BJS, 1987b) of 3,995 parolees between the ages of seventeen and twenty-two indicated that 69% of them were rearrested for a serious crime within six years of their release. Among other findings, "these parolees were arrested for more than 36,000 new felonies or serious misdemeanors, including approximately 6,700 violent crimes and nearly 19,000 property crimes" (p. 1). Also, the longer the prior arrest record and the earlier the first adult arrest, the more likely the chance of recidivism. The amount of time served in prison had no influence on the recidivism rate.

As a treatment, therefore, imprisonment doesn't seem to cure much.

PRISONER OR PATIENT

Twenty-two years of experience proved that the Defective Delinquency Law was unworkable. Whether or not it was a "good" law, it was an unpopular law: Patuxent had the dubious distinction of being the most sued institution in the United States. And whether or not the treatment program actually worked seemed more a matter of opinion than fact. Even a friend of Patuxent's, Peter Lejins (1977), answered "No" to the question, "Has Patuxent contributed anything new to treatment?" Lejins accurately pointed out that *every* treatment approach used at Patuxent had been used someplace else before. True, but even the hypercritical CRC *Report* had to conclude that Patuxent did a better job of rehabilitation than the conventional prison. For in fact, Patuxent *did* contribute something new to the treatment of criminality. No *one* treatment approach—psychotherapy, behavior modification, education, etc.—was likely to be effective, but all occurring together in a humane environment under the direction of mental health professionals, the total treatment approach, *was* new in a correctional setting, and in this regard Patuxent is still different from any other correctional setting in the United States.

One can't escape the fact that Patuxent is unique and that most prisons simply do not have the mental health manpower, the adaquate physical plant, or the special law which facilitates treatment. In most prisons prisoners never do become patients, but the Patuxent "laboratory" is valueless if the results can't be generalized to other settings. To label "prisoner" or "patient" doesn't really change anything, except that one label is perjorative and the other benign, and they reflect how we think rather than describe who we're talking about. On the one hand, perhaps, we're punishing the bad person, while on the other we're treating a sick person. I believe this is one of those dichotomies which need not exist. To treat is not to ignore morality, but rather is to include the moral nature of the individual as a part of a psychodynamic system. Punishment is not alien to treatment, but punishment alone is bad treatment.

Over the last thirty years the Patuxent experience has taught that criminals aren't all alike, that heroic measures are needed to treat some, that some don't need treatment at all, that some will become noncriminal no matter what you do, and that some are apparently incurable. However, among chronic criminals there are some common themes which transcend most demographic and diagnostic variables, themes which give us insight into the nature of criminality and which suggest treatment strategies, be the criminal prisoner or patient, or the setting prison-like or hospital-like.

2
Crime and Criminality

After a comprehensive examination of the literature on criminal behavior, Wilson and Herrnstein (1985) state that the only statistically reliable conclusion from the evidence is that criminals tend to be young males. Nonetheless, they go on to espouse a biogenetic theory of criminality which includes such traits as race, low intelligence, and body build. These conclusions are questioned by Kamin (1986), who particularly attacks their somatotype inferences. It is true, for example, that delinquents and criminals tend to have predominantly mesomorphic physiques; however, it is also true that the majority of the male population in the same age range also have predominantly mesomorphic physiques. As for tested intelligence, considering the whole gamut of cultural, socioeconomic, and emotional disruptions in the life history of the average criminal, there is reason to question the validity of IQ scores. With respect to race, the undisputed fact is that in 1983 blacks, who were 12% of the general U.S. population, were 39% of the jail inmate population (BJS, 1985). Wilson and Herrnstein are careful to say, "there's no reason to believe that the genes determining one's skin pigmentation also affect criminality" (p. 29), but genes do determine physique and intelligence, and black men are found to be more mesomorphic and less intelligent than white men, so they are more genetically "disposed" toward criminal behavior. Socioeconomic conditions also play a role of course, but the authors also demonstrate the genetic inferiority of the lower classes. Kamin points out that the authors were careful to select research findings which would support their views while ignoring the wide body of contradictory research findings.

A knowledge of the demographics of crime probably tell us little or nothing about the nature of criminality. For example, the FBI (1985) reports that in 1984 50.5% of all persons arrested were under the age of twenty-five though the mode (17%) was age range twenty-five through twenty-nine for both males and females. Males accounted for 83.3% of all persons arrested. Other data tell us that proportionately men and blacks are more often arrested for violent crimes than women and whites, and there is more crime in urban than rural areas. All of which is perfectly predictable: young, city-bred, black males are more likely than anyone else to be arrested. Looked at demographically, it might indeed be fair to say that age, race, and gender—perhaps even IQ and physique—are the key determinants of the single criminal act, but it's not fair to say they are the determinants of criminality.

In Chapter 1 we looked at the diagnostic distinctions between jail and prison inmates, and I think these distinctions suggest that we're talking about two different populations when we talk about the "arrested" and the "incarcerated." That is, while virtually anybody is capable of the single criminal act, criminality goes beyond acts to become a psychodynamic process.

The distinction between crime and criminality must be made if society is ever to protect itself adequately, and so far society has been unwilling to do that. We have instead made moral assumptions about all criminal behavior which may not in fact be valid. That is, we assume that the individual commits crimes because he's "bad" and that he will no longer be a criminal when he learns to be "good." So we punish him to induce him to be "good," and if that doesn't work, then we punish him more severely. Society seems convinced that the individual can make that change from "bad" to "good" if only he wants to. This assumption forms the basis for Wilson and Herrnstein's theory of criminality, that the biogenetic predisposition toward crime can be controlled by the individual who inevitably has free choice. They say:

> At any given moment, a person can choose between committing a crime and not committing it (all these alternatives to crime we lump together as "noncrime"). The consequences of committing the crime consist of rewards . . . and punishments; the consequences of not committing the crime (i.e. engaging in noncrime) also entail gains and losses. The larger the ratio of the net rewards of crime to the net rewards of noncrime, the greater the tendency to commit the crime. The net rewards of crime include, obviously, the

likely material gains from the crime, but they also include intangible benefits, such as obtaining emotional or sexual gratification, receiving the approval of peers, satisfying an old score against an enemy, or enhancing one's sense of justice. One must deduct from these rewards of crime any losses that accrue immediately—that are, so to speak, contemporaneous with the crime. They include the pangs of conscience, the disapproval of onlookers, and the retaliation of the victim. (p. 44)

All of this is later nicely conceptualized in a mathematical model which reduces human beings to plusses and minuses. So thinking, we can't avoid making moral judgments.

If there is a distinction between criminal behavior, which may indeed be a moral issue, and criminality as a psychodynamic process, where there is criminality the "net rewards" of crime may not be obvious and the motivation for crime not necessarily deliberate amorality. To take this view does not relieve the individual of his responsibility for his criminal acts, but it does suggest the possibility of personality variables which punishment may not affect.

DETERMINANTS OF CRIMINALITY

In any prison we are likely to find the criminal who has committed the "bad" act but who is not a "bad" person. Jean Harris (1986), the woman who murdered the "Scarsdale Diet" doctor, is a good example. She was headmistress of the exclusive Madeira School in Virginia before—in what must be considered a crime of passion—she shot Dr. Herman Tarnower, and she is now serving fifteen years to life in prison. In cases like this one wonders at society's single-minded determination to punish since it is unlikely that Ms. Harris, who never committed a crime before, will ever commit a crime again, no matter how many years she spends in prison, even if she never went to prison. Society's answer may be that her example serves as a deterrent for others, but I doubt that the individual human being is really capable of making that association when he's caught up in the emotionally overwhelming situation. I don't mean to infer that Ms. Harris and others like her should be excused or that we should take lightly the murder of anyone, but I wonder that these people should bear the same label "criminal" as the men and women who have spent their lives committing criminal acts, and I wonder that they're all treated the same way.

People like Ms. Harris are perhaps the exceptions in the prison system. Let me illustrate a more common type of "criminal" with the case of Paul, who served time in a conventional prison, and who I didn't meet until after he was placed on parole. He was referred to outpatient psychotherapy on the assumption that he was potentially violent, which in fact he wasn't. Treatment may have helped him, but I suspect he would have done just as well without it.

Paul was a 28 year old black man who was on parole, having served 5 years of a 10 year sentence for robbery. This was his only felony conviction, though he had numerous arrests for such offenses as disorderly conduct and gambling. Paul frankly admitted that he drank too much and that he used marijuana, but he adamantly denied the use of other drugs. He believed he'd be all right if he just drank beer; it was the whiskey that made him "crazy." He blamed the felony conviction on whiskey. "I don't steal," he declared. "I'm not a thief." He went on to express contempt for men who did steal, and the worst part of prison, he implied, was his forced association with "bad company." Paul said he and some buddies got drunk, and it was his buddies who decided to hold up a gas station. "I was passed out in the back seat of the car," he said. "I didn't know a robbery was going down."

"You mean," I asked him, "if you had been conscious you would have walked away?"

"I'd have wanted to." But maybe he wouldn't. He could admit that keeping the good opinion of his buddies was important.

Paul went to live with his mother when he got out of prison, and he and his mother's current live-in boyfriend got to be good drinking buddies, and his mother drank right along with them. These were good times. He didn't always have a job, but he was always sure of a bed, food, and beer in his mother's home. Then a younger brother came home from prison and everything changed. "He think he a badassed little motherfucker," Paul said. Well, the mother preferred the younger son, he caused trouble between mother and boyfriend, the boyfriend moved out, and dope pushers started to move in. Little brother was a hustler, and, as Paul put it, "Every day some new shit. I get home from work yesterday and there's cops sitting in the kitchen. What I know about a murder, they ask me. You read about it in the *Sun?* This dealer what was shot over on Broadway? Shit! I don't know about no murder. My brother, he know, but I ain't gonna tell the cops that."

At about this time Paul found himself a woman, and he moved in with her. Her name was Shirley, and as Paul told it, he was in love for the first time in his life. He would have married Shirley except that she already had a husband, who was in jail, and who was due to be released in just a few months. "What then?" I asked Paul. "You know he can't just let you walk off with his woman. He's got to do something."

Well, Paul would worry about that later. In the meantime, he was laid-off again, broke, and he was being supported by both Shirley and his mother. That bothered him because he didn't feel like a man when he was taking money from women. But no matter how hard I tried to convince him to save money when he was working, knowing that lay-offs were coming, he just wouldn't. *Give* his money to a bank! Money he couldn't feel in his pocket didn't belong to him.

By now Shirley's husband was about to get out of jail, so Paul moved back in with his mother. Little brother was locked up again.

"And what about Shirley?" I asked.

"Her husband, he won't stay with her long. He come home and knock her around a little bit, then he be gone. Then Shirl and me get together again."

"You don't think the guy will come looking for you?"

"Maybe." He wouldn't look at me.

"You got a piece?"

"I'm on parole, Doc. What you do I tell you I got a piece?"

As luck would have it, the husband didn't give a damn about Paul, and true to Paul's prediction, he knocked Shirley around a little bit and then deserted her. But another man got into her bed before Paul could get back. . . .

Paul moved from adventure to adventure, always just skirting the fringes of crime and violence, and in the end, when his therapy was terminated, he was still crime-free and still unsettled. Throughout his story there are the themes of heavy drinking, dependency on women, inability to plan ahead, avoidance of responsibility, impulsive pleasure seeking, and acceptance of the ghetto code of honor. Yet this was a man who declared proudly, "I ain't no thief and I ain't no junkie." Paul is presented here as a not atypical criminal from the ghetto, one of those FBI statistics, who became neither more or less criminal because of his prison experience.

Criminality cannot be inferred just because the person committed a criminal act. I doubt that anyone believes that Ms. Harris really has a criminal nature, though society in general may think less kindly of Paul. Criminality goes beyond the act. Consider the following case, Dexter, who was born and brought up in roughly the same neighborhood as Paul.

Dexter, an 18 year old black male, was serving a life sentence for robbery and felony-murder. This was his first conviction as an adult, but he had an extensive history of juvenile delinquency.

Dexter was the third of seven children born to his mother, the first male child, and the only child fathered by Mr. M, who soon after Dexter was born was killed in a shoot-out with police officers. When Dexter was five years old, a Mr. White moved into the home, and though Dexter's mother calls herself Mrs. White, there was never a legal marriage. Dexter was encouraged to call Mr. White "Daddy," but to Dexter Mr. White has always been "Mr. White." Though Mr. White is a hard working, reliable family man, Dexter hates him. He says Mr. White physically abused him while he was growing up. Mrs. White denies this. She says her husband tried to discipline Dexter, and the boy never did anything but rebel. She says Dexter was always "hard to handle."

Dexter was a problem in school. He was bright enough, but he was known as a child who "wants his own way all the time." His juvenile record started at about age eight with truancy and shoplifting, and by age ten he was committed to the training school. A year later he was home again, but he was just as rebellious as ever. He responded to Mr. White's discipline by stabbing him with a pen-knife and running away from home. Apprehended, he was returned to the training school, from which he promptly escaped. By the age of 17 he had been arrested for a variety of crimes, including stealing, assault, warehouse-breaking, and dope peddling. He never attempted an honest job. Eventually he and a companion tried to rob a liquor store, the proprietor resisted, and he was shot and killed.

"I didn't shoot him, man," Dexter said to me. "My rap-partner shot him. I don't deserve no life sentence. I got an appeal in."

I think it apparent that there's a lot going on inside Dexter that isn't related to his culture. Criminal behavior may be related to social learning experiences, but it isn't dependent on them. In fact, Paul is by far the more typical ghetto product, for this is a sub-culture which encourages escapist though essentially non-criminal behavior. These "escapes" include such things as excessive use of alcohol; dependency on marijuana and other "soft" drugs; gambling, particularly legal lotteries on which large parts of pay-packets may be squandered; magical beliefs, including religiosity, magic numbers, and "roots" and other forms of voodoo; sexual promiscuity; and "suit-cases," the dream of making large sums of money by suing anyone and everyone for real and imagined harms.

These, not criminality, are the characteristics of the people of the ghetto.

Cultural influences on behavior cannot be denied. In Baltimore there is a conclave of Lombard Indians, a branch of the Cherokee Nation. The men in these families are usually hard workers; they have a particular talent for working in high places such as building skyscrapers or painting the Chesapeake Bay Bridge, and though they are very well paid for their work, their families often live near the poverty level because of rampant alcoholism. Fights in their neighborhood bars are a common occurrence, and every now and then one of these fights ends with a death. I've treated several of these "murderers" with roughly the same result: an almost passive acceptance of the prison milieu, model behavior, impenetrable defenses in the course of psychotherapy, and a return to exactly the same life style when set free. Treatment was a waste of time, and in another sense, imprisonment was a waste of time. It wasn't just that these men didn't believe they were murderers, neither did their families and friends, and neither did the family and friends of the victim. The drinking and the fights were culturally approved; the death was an accident. A distinction exists between criminal behavior and criminal intent, and in criminality there is always intent.

The influence of culture, though, need not be restricted to ethnic minorities. In a brief review of criminology theory, discussing morality and crime, Empey (1985) has this to say:

> These old time moralists also contended that Americans wanted to have their cake and eat it too; that is, to be protected from crime, yet to be unfettered in their own pursuit of wealth and property. Indeed, it was this drive for autonomy and property that had led to the colonization of America, to slavery, to the genocide of the Indians, and that continues to fuel the engines of America's prosperity. Hence, said (Bell), "Crime is an American way of life." And Sutherland had the temerity to suggest "that it is difficult to imagine a respectable philosophy which would be more in harmony with, and conducive to criminality, than the individualistic philosophy upon which American democracy is built." (p. 5)

Perhaps it is this peculiarly American ethic which accounts for white-collar crime particularly, and in recent years Americans have even ceased to be shocked when criminal behavior and *intent* have been demonstrated even at the level of the presidency. That "all politicians are crooked anyhow" is one of America's enduring myths, and cheating on one's income tax is almost a national habit. There are few of us in fact who have not intentionally behaved in a criminal way, even if only by exceeding the speed limit. However, while the *criminal act* and the *criminal intent* are both requisites of criminality, both may be in the behavioral repertoire of noncriminal people. Criminality, on the other hand, may be considered to be the individual's characteristic mode of interpersonal activity.

To further consider the distinction between crime and criminality, let's take a brief look at certain biogenetic factors, particularly physique, since this aspect has been the subject of many studies, and the results clearly indicate that delinquents and criminals are mainly mesomorphs. Because one can explain away these results (as Kamin did) doesn't prove that they have no meaning. Just as there are sociocultural influences on behavior, there are also biogenetic influences. The mistake is to call the influence the cause. We will later (Chapter 3) take a look at the psychophysiology of psychopaths and note that they are different from the norm, and while this difference may play a role in their social adaptation, it is not the cause of antisocial acting out. However, when we look at any human behavior, we start with the physical human being, a biological organism in dialogue with its environment. On the most elementary level, the fat boy and the hollow-chested skeleton can't run fast or far, so they're not as likely as the athletic mesomorph to play "catch me" games with the police, and they're not so likely to test their physical strength in violent confrontations. But more important are the tempermental correlates of body build, the phlegmaticism of the endomorph, the hypersensitivity of the ectomorph, and the stimulus-hunger of the mesomorph. There *is* a biological dimension of behavior which we'd be foolish to ignore. Let me illustrate with two cases.

Billy was a handsome boy, six-three, two hundred and twenty pounds of well-proportioned muscle, the pride of his family, and adored by all the girls. His parents had humble origins, but his mother was now a school teacher and his father was a GS-12 with the Social Security Administration. An upwardly mobile black family, the parents placed strong emphasis on achievement and conformity. All of their children were either bright or talented. Billy's IQ was only average, but with his physique and muscular coordination he was an extraordinary athlete. The quarterback of his high school football team in his junior year, he was scouted by several colleges, a scholarship was assured, and a career in professional football a possibility. Then he was injured in an automobile accident, his spine was damaged, and he was told that any new injury might cause permanent paralysis. He did graduate from high school, but he had no natural academic ability, he wasn't interested in college, and there was no job he wanted to do. That summer after graduation he started to associate with a "bad crowd," he started drinking, and his new friends "turned him on" to heroin. By the end of the summer he had participated in three armed robberies, and he was eventually sentenced to 25 years in prison.

Treating Billy, it soon became apparent to me that his criminal behavior was ego-dystonic. The accident which had wiped out his potential career in sports had not wiped out his value system, and his criminal behavior might well be understood in terms of a reactive depression. In fact, we rarely focused on the acts which brought him to prison; we focused instead on that part of his ego, the greater part, which was still healthy. He did have an identity beyond that of the "football hero," and the task was to help him find it an accept it. Within a relatively brief time Billy was returned to the community where he continued in therapy as an outpatient, and he never committed another crime.

The next young man is quite a different story.

Roy was a magnificent specimen of the young male animal: tall, powerfully built, and extraordinarily handsome. His parents said he was "big" when he was born, and through every stage of his life he was bigger and more powerful than his age-mates, and throughout his life he tended to bully and dominate others. Seeing him with his parents, it was apparent that his mother adored him in an almost sexual way, and his father was afraid of him. Roy used their feelings to control them, and I could guess that these had been the family dynamics for many years. Roy had been in trouble for most of his life, starting with aggressive behavior while he was still in kindergarten, on through fights and disobedience in elementary school, and finally an assault on a teacher when he was in junior high, a behavior which finally got him expelled from public school and into the purview of the juvenile court. There followed years of treatment, training schools, and escalating delinquent behavior, until at the age of 17 he was waived to the adult court as the result of an armed robbery. Prison held no terrors for him; he was unbeatable in any fight. In therapy, he tried to either bully or charm his therapist, but he never became anxious enough to change. Eventually he was released from prison on a technicality, and soon after he committed another string of armed robberies which brought him back to prison for many years.

I have little doubt that their physical being contributed to the criminal behavior of both Billy and Roy, that because of physique and tempearment they were both prone to solve problems through actions. But beyond the physical they were two quite different boys. Billy grew up in an emotionally healthy family that offered firm values and support; while Roy's aggression was never channeled, he was allowed to "grow out of control," and his belief in himself as someone special, for whom the rules do not apply, was reinforced by his mother's unnatural love and his father's unnatural fear.

In the course of their treatment I asked them something like this: "How does it feel to be physically superior to the average man?" The answer was in part predictable since in adolescents body-image and self-concept are so closely linked, but additionally, both these boys let me know that they felt inferior along every dimension other than the physical. The adjectives I used to describe them—*powerful* physique, *magnificent* specimen—were adjectives everyone used to describe them, the way others automatically responded to them, and they became "creatures" who were envied by less endowed men, the threat in rough-and-tumble adolescence, and the sex object of adoring females. They couldn't get beyond their bodies but neither could anyone else. There was that dialogue with the environment.

To continue with biology, it is often proposed that the sexual criminal is biologically "different" and that this accounts for his criminal behavior (see Chapter 7). In some cases this may be true, he may be genotypically or biochemically different, there may exist in him the tendency to commit a sexual crime, his dialogue with the environment may be outside the norm, but I cannot agree that any of this accounts for his criminality. For along with the criminal *act* and criminal *intent*, criminality also includes the *willingness* to engage in repetitive criminal behavior, and sexual criminals tend to be repeaters. Often included in the biogenetic explanation is the concept of sexual addiction (e.g., Carnes, 1983) which, like other addictions, eventually takes over and controls the individual's life. However, to infer an obsessive-compulsive mechanism to sexual deviancy does not account for criminal behavior. No addiction, no deviance, is *per se* criminal; it is the transgression, the act in defiance of law, that is criminal. While there is certainly a psychodynamic difference between the bank robber and the child molester, in the end their willingness to transgress may make them more alike than different.

The following is the case of a child molester, a man who I examined but never treated. I think you'll see why.

Harry is a 70 year old white male who is serving a sentence of 50 years for 10 counts of child sexual abuse. He is a college graduate, a widower, and he claims a history of high salaried positions with many consulting firms. This is doubtful considering the many times he has been incarcerated, but he presents himself as a silver-haired executive type, urbane and dignified in spite of his prison grays.

His criminal record starts in Georgia in 1947 when he was charged with multiple counts of sodomy, for which he was placed on probation and referred to outpatient treatment. While in treatment he sodomized several more boys, he fled from the state before a warrant could be served, and for some reason the state didn't go after him. He was next arrested and convicted in Indiana for 14 counts of sodomy, and he received a 20 year prison sentence. He served 10 years before he made parole, and then he moved to Pennsylvania, where in 1965 he was again convicted of multiple sexual offenses involving young boys. He served another 5 years, and after his release he moved to Maryland. In 1972 he was again convicted of sodomy, placed on probation, and referred for treatment. He was placed on antiandrogenic medication, but in 1973 he was again arrested for sodomy. This time he received a 15 year prison sentence, but he was released on parole in 1982. Six months later he was arrested for the instant offense.

When he left prison the last time Harry moved in with his daughter and her two teenage sons. He sodomized them. These boys introduced him to their friends, ranging in age from 10 to 14, and he sodomized them. He established a "clubhouse" for the neighborhood boys where he took sexually explicit photographs of them and made pornographic films. His adventures came to an end when one unwilling boy complained to his parents.

During an interview with me Harry complained about the injustice of his sentence. "I need treatment, Doc," he said. "I shouldn't be in prison."

Considering a man like Harry, it's awfully difficult to avoid taking a moral stance, for in the course of a lifetime he molested literally hundreds of boys, including even his own grandsons. We think: How consumate this evil! Yet one wonders at the strength and persistence of his aberrant sexual drive, and one prefers to believe that this must be mental illness. Over the years the law and psychiatry dealt with Harry first one way and then another, punishing him through incarcerations, or trying treatments from behavior modification to psychoanalysis and including chemical castration along the way. In the end, when a judge sentenced a seventy year old man to fifty years in prison, the judge admitted the failure of everything law and psychiatry has to offer. When the professional staff at Patuxent later refused to treat, they agreed with the judge.

Presenting the contrasting cases of Paul and Dexter and Billy and Roy, I have attempted to illustrate the proposition that criminal behavior and criminality are not synonymous. Paul's criminal behavior was almost accidental, and Billy would never have been induced to commit crimes if he hadn't been so depressed; but both Dexter and Roy were cold and uncaring men who didn't hesitate to use and hurt others to satisfy their needs. Paul and Billy were punished once and that was more than enough to cure them; but Dexter and Roy returned again and again to punishment as moths drawn to a flame. Harry, in his own way, isn't much different from Dexter and Roy. Our prisons are full of men like Harry, Dexter, and Roy; they're chronic criminals.

I believe prison populations can be divided into two broad categories, which for the moment I'll call chronic criminals and "others." The "others" are men like Paul and Billy for whom imprisonment is probably a curative experience; which doesn't mean that I think there should be no other treatment for them or that they should be subjected to the prevailing inhumane prison conditions; they can be destroyed as well as cured. These "others" are basically not society's problem, and to a large extent they aren't psychiatry's problem either; most logically, they should be the paramount concern of corrections, which has the obligation to provide them with the best possible rehabilitative experience (in this best of all possible worlds). The chronic criminals *are* society's problem and *should be* psychiatry's, for these are the recidivists, the predators, for whom neither law, psychiatry, nor corrections has yet found an answer. I suspect there will always be men like Harry who, with either sadness or anger, we must consign to permanent imprisonment, but that leaves a lot of others who, whether we like it or not, will be free again someday. And they will commit more crimes.

It's not my purpose here to document horrible prison conditions. Many others (e.g., Clark, 1970; Menninger, 1968; Mitford, 1971) have undertaken that task, with unfortunately little impact on correctional practice in the United States. Essentially, there can be little doubt that imprisonment is designed to be a punishing experience. But what if it isn't? What if the very conditions we deplore are the ones prisoners seek to perpetuate? Reformers have always attacked the system from the outside in, which attempts have generally failed. It might make more sense to start with the prisoners, for it is here that the inertia, the resistance to change, is greatest. I'll have more to say about the prisoner society later (Chapter 4), but one thing is dramatically clear: that society is self-perpetuating. By extension, that which we deem to be punishing may be rewarding instead. Clark said that our prisons produce criminals, but it might be more accurate to say that our prisons produce prisoners.

Now we arrive at the last difference between crime and criminality. There is the criminal *act*, criminal *intent*, a *willingness* to repeat the criminal act, and finally *indifference to punishment*. These concepts don't mean that the individual doesn't suffer when he's in prison; he may, but for whatever reason the suffering is not only tolerable, it may also be preferable to freedom. For example, I recall hearing a group of black men discussing their experiences as juvenile delinquents, how they planned their incarcerations in the training school: some said they always aimed for the winter months so they wouldn't have to go to public schools; others said the summer months were better, the training school becoming a substitute for summer camp. For these men, whatever the intent of the court when it incarcerated them, they had their own agenda.

On an intellectual level it may be easy to understand how poor black boys who lived in slum conditions may have preferred the clean rooms and the good food of the training school to the impoverished homes they came from, even if they had to give up some personal freedom to attain it. In terms of pure learning theory, an operant conditioning paradigm, one might appreciate how the behavior was reinforced and perpetuated even into adulthood. But then something goes radically wrong with the intellectual approach, for now we have men who blithely speak of their "vacations on the street" between incarcerations. Imprisonment—in even the so-called "country club" prisons, and there aren't many like that—means *loss* of personal autonomy, *loss* of heterosexual relations, and *loss* of self-direction, all those daily restrictions on movement, choice, and self-determination which add up to *loss* of freedom. The ordinary law-breaker is shattered by the whole process of arrest, trial, conviction, and sentence even before imprisonment, his shame is bared to family and friends, his self-respect hangs in tatters, and feelings of utter worthlessness may consume him as the prison doors clang shut behind him. But the chronic criminal, though chained hand and foot, returns to prison with a big grin on his face, a cheery greeting for everyone, eager to get to his tier with his home-boys for an exchange of the latest gossip; in effect, he breathes a sigh of relief to be home again.

The above is not an exaggeration for dramatic effect; it really happens that way. Just as typically though, the smiling man will complain that it's a "bum rap," the judge and jury were prejudiced, his lawyer was incompetent, and he's going to appeal. Sometimes the affect even goes along with the words, particularly if there was some impropriety during the trial even though guilt is indisputable, for our chronic criminals insist that others play by the rules even though they do not. One gets the sense that it's all a game, and whatever the intent of society when it imposed a prison sentence, somehow the prisoner has won the game.

SUMMARY AND SYNTHESIS

Criminality cannot be said to exist unless all four of these element are present. To consider each of them again:

There must be a criminal *act*. So saying, we can eliminate many instances of behavioral problems, such as juvenile status offenses—running away from home, truancy, etc.—and some adult misdemeanors, such as drunk in public and vagrancy. Problems like these may be precursors of criminal behavior or may co-exist with criminal behaviors, but they are not *per se* indicators of criminality. However, the act may be fairly passive, such as aiding and abetting in the commission of a crime or knowingly buying stolen merchandise. Essentially, we make a distinction here between disruptive behaviors and those which are unquestionably deliberate violations of law.

There must be criminal *intent*. The man who goes out drinking with his buddies, who gets in a fight, and who kills his victim did not set out that day to commit homicide, but he did. Or the man who gets a little too rough with his girlfriend in the back seat of his car did not set out that day to rape, but he raped. It's not unusual for men who lead relatively loose, amoral lives to wander into situations of dire consequence; the mechanism, though, is lack of foresight and judgment, not criminal intent. However, intent *can* be inferred when an unplanned major crime grows out of deliberate minor criminal behavior. For example, the dope addict buying his supply and the drunk who drives are both consciously breaking the law; if the addict later kills in a PCP frenzy and the drunk runs over a pedestrian, we can't say that either intended to commit homicide specifically, but both are still intentional criminals.

There must be a *willingness* to repeat the criminal act. The drunk driver in the above example, for instance, if he is the ordinary man with a drinking problem, will likely be so appalled by the consequences of his behavior that he may never drink and drive again, which is not the same as saying that he will never drink again. If the man continues to drink and drive, then he is not just an alcoholic; there is probably a criminal part of his personality which may be associated with his addiction, but it is a problem different from his addiction. Willingness, though, doesn't just mean returning to crime after punishment, it also means repetitive criminal behavior before any sanctions are imposed. White-collar criminals and gangland members often fall into this category; they tend to be different from other criminals in terms of the extraordinary pains they take to avoid being caught.

The first three of these elements, therefore, account for most of the "others" in prisons. They include deliberate law-breakers whose behavior will probably change as the result of their experiences in the criminal justice system, the "accidental" major violators who may still be relatively amoral upon release but who have little bent for crime, the one-time offender whose criminal behavior was an aberration in an otherwise healthy personality, and certain career criminals who may be relatively successful at crime and who strive to avoid incarceration. Since they rarely recidivate, we can estimate that these "others" represent about a third of the prison population. The remaining two-thirds do recidivate, they are apparently *indifferent to punishment,* and that is the hallmark of criminality. Most of these men will also be called antisocial personalities.

Criminality is not the same as psychopathy but they are very alike. Of both chronic criminals and psychopaths we can say, "They have a will to fail."

3
An Unhurried View of Psychopathy

Few statements about the antisocial personality are more true than the opening paragraph of Reid's (1981) discussion of the syndrome:

> The phrase "antisocial personality" represents the most used diagnostic concept in forensic psychiatry and one of the most common syndrome stereotypes in general psychiatry and psychology. Even with increasing efforts towards specific syndrome definition in the mental health professions, it seems safe to say that each clinical or forensic professional has his or her own definition of antisocial personality, as well as a set of impressions—often derived from extensive experience—regarding treatment and prognosis. (p. 133)

The various diagnostic and statistical manuals of the American Psychiatric Association have struggled with the syndrome, and at this point in time the terms "psychopath," "sociopath," and "antisocial personality" are used almost interchangeably. I prefer the term "psychopath," for this word implies a disturbance of cognition rather than of behavior,

33

a condition which exists outside of the interpersonal situation and which colors the individual's approach to all of life.

THE DIAGNOSIS OF PSYCHOPATHY

In the classical sense of the term, a distinction between psychopathy and antisocial behavior can be made. Kozol (1959) writes:

> Some generalizations about the psychopath may be in order. He is, at one and the same time, the blessing and the bane of society. Without him there would be little if any art, literature, music or science—or crime. One does not *have* to be a psychopath to be a creator or a criminal, but it helps. He is the problem child of society, and although easy to recognize is difficult to define. . . .
>
> Is there any difference between legal nonconformity and artistic or literary or even academic nonconformity? I doubt if there is. In my opinion there is no basic difference between the psychopath who enriches society and the one who robs it: they are cut of the same cloth, and any apparent difference is in their goals rather than in their substance. (p. 637)

Again in the classic interpretation of the term, there is also a distinction between the antisocial psychopath and the criminal. Cleckley (1959) says the criminal differs from the psychopath in that he is (1) more goal-oriented, that his criminal behavior is purposive, and that there is a potential for tangible reward from his criminal acts; (2) he is more consistent in making efforts to avoid and avoiding the consequences of his criminal behavior; and (3) he is capable of maintaining loyalty to persons, groups, and codes. Accepting that distinction, we'll find very few nonpsychopathic chronic criminals in prison.

In Chapter 1 we looked at the diagnoses of prisoners, and it was found that roughly 85% could be diagnosed among the personality disorders, of whom about 50% were antisocial personalities. One may question if today's "antisocial personality" is equivalent to yesterday's "psychopath," particularly as the psychopath was described by Cleckley (1964), a description which by now may be considered classic. The classic psychopath has these enduring traits:

1. Superficial charm and good intelligence.
2. Absence of delusions and other signs of irrational thinking.
3. Absence of nervousness or psychoneurotic manifestations.
4. Unreliability.

5. Untruthfulness and insincerity.
6. Lack of remorse or shame.
7. Inadequately motivated antisocial behavior.
8. Poor judgment and failure to learn by experience.
9. Pathological egocentricity and incapacity for love.
10. General poverty in major affective reactions.
11. Specific loss of insight.
12. Unresponsiveness in general interpersonal relations.
13. Fantastic and uninviting behavior with drink and sometimes without.
14. Suicide rarely carried out.
15. Sex life impersonal, trivial, and poorly integrated.
16. Failure to follow any life plan.

The Cleckley definition places little emphasis on crime *per se*, and the illustrations he offers in *The Mask of Sanity* are largely noncriminal patients. They get into all kinds of trouble, no doubt, and they commit criminal acts, but their criminal behavior is poorly motivated, not purposive, and almost an artifact of their disastrous interpersonal relationships. Through all the editions of *The Mask of Sanity* Cleckley insisted on the distinction between psychopathic and criminal behavior, but in recent years that diagnostic distinction seems to have faded.

Let's consider the American Psychiatric Association's (APA) diagnostic and statistical manuals' definitions over the years, calling them for conveniences sake DSM-I (APA, 1952), DSM-II (APA, 1968), and DSM-III (APA, 1980).

DSM-I defined as a broad category Sociopathic Personality Disturbance with four sub-categories: Antisocial Reaction, Dyssocial Reaction, Sexual Deviation, and Addiction. The sociopath in general was considered to be "ill primarily in terms of society and of conformity with the prevailing cultural milieu, and not only in terms of personal discomfort and relations with other individuals" (p. 38). The subcategory Antisocial Reaction, as defined below, included cases previously defined as psychopathic personality.

This term refers to chronically antisocial individuals who are always in trouble, profiting from neither experience nor punishment, and maintaining no real loyalties to any person, group, or code. They are frequently callous and hedonistic, showing marked emotional immaturity, with lack of sense of responsibility, lack of judgment, and an ability to rationalize their behavior so that it appears warranted, reasonable, and justified. (p. 38.)

DSM-I attempted to make a distinction between psychopathy and criminal behavior in its definition of Dyssocial Reaction: "These individuals typically do not show personality deviations other than those implied by adherence to the values or code of their own predatory, criminal, or other social group" (p. 38). The term Sexual Deviation was meant to include "most of the cases formerly classed as 'psychopathic personality with pathologic sexuality'" (p. 39).

Thus, DSM-I adhered very closely to the classic definition of psychopathy, there was recognition that there was more than one kind of psychopath, and all criminals weren't called psychopathic. Similarly, DSM-II made a distinction between psychopathy and criminal behavior. It defined Dyssocial behavior as follows: "This category is for individuals who are not classifiable as antisocial personalities, but who are predatory and follow more or less criminal pursuits, such as racketeers, dishonest gamblers, prostitutes, and dope peddlers" (p. 52).

The DSM-II definition of Antisocial Personality continued to be very like the classical definition of psychopathy:

> They are incapable of significant loyalty to individuals, groups, or social values. They are grossly selfish, callous, irresponsible, impulsive, and unable to feel guilt or to learn from experience and punishment. Frustration tolerance is low. They tend to blame others or offer plausible rationalizations for their behavior. *A mere history of repeated legal or social offenses is not sufficient to justify this diagnosis* [italics added]. (p. 43)

By the time we get to DSM-III all that has changed. The Antisocial Personality is now defined as a disorder "in which there is a history of continual and chronic antisocial behavior in which the rights of others are violated" (p. 317). Now little attempt is made to distinguish between the classic psychopath and the ordinary criminal. As close as DSM-III comes is in the V Code category of Adult Antisocial Behavior, which is too narrowly defined to include yesterday's "Dyssocial Reaction."

With respect to the diagnosis of prisoners, therefore, the question is this: Are all those antisocial personalities in our prisons classic psychopaths, or aren't they? A study by Hare (1983) perhaps sheds some light on the matter.

Hare's subjects were 246 white male prison inmates who had been diagnosed (DSM-III criteria) Antisocial Personality Disorder. These subjects were reevaluated using a psychopathy checklist of twenty-two items based on Cleckley's work. These twenty-two items could be reduced to five sets of interrelated factors:

> ... 1) impulsive, unstable life style with no long-term commitments, 2) callousness and lack of empathy, guilt, remorse, or concern for others, 3) superficial interpersonal relationships, 4) early appearance of chronic antisocial behavior, and 5) inadequately motivated criminal acts. (p. 888)

Hare found that there was a significant correlation between the diagnosis of Antisocial Personality Disorder and the assessment of psychopathy *in the prison population*. He commented that "DSM-III does not readily identify individuals who may fit the classic picture of psychopathy but who manage, for one reason or another, to avoid early or frequent contact with the judicial system" (p. 889). In another study, Hare (1985) compared procedures for assessing psychopathy in several settings, and he again concluded that while DSM-III places too much emphasis on criminal behavior, the diagnosis of Antisocial Personality Disorder does tend to identify the classic psychopath.

IDIOPATHIC AND SYMPTOMATIC PSYCHOPATHY

Though Hare's work is only suggestive, perhaps we can assume that the *traits* of the classic psychopath exist in the chronic criminal. That is, we move from diagnosis to phenomenology. It has been suggested (Persons, 1986) that diagnostic-category-studies result in a misclassification of individuals, while a symptom-approach studies important phenomena which are ignored by the diagnostic-category design and contribute to the development of psychological theory. Indeed, long ago Karpman (1941, 1948) suggested that psychopathic personality was a myth, that if we studied psychopathic behavior long enough we'd probably find a better diagnosis. He also suggested that of those called psychopaths there are probably two distinct types, the primary or idiopathic, and the secondary or symptomatic. A typology of this sort may help to distinguish between chronic criminals, particularly as we evaluate the effects of social learning experiences. Let me illustrate with the cases of two black men who were in their early twenties when they were examined.

> Brian is serving a total sentence of 15 years for Robbery With A Deadly Weapon (2 counts), Handgun Violation (2 counts), Assault, and Malicious Destruction of Property. He says this is the first time he has used a weapon in the commission of a crime, and the record

indicates that these are the most aggravated crimes he has ever committed. He has a record of 15 juvenile arrests and 10 adult arrests, generally for misdemeanors. He has served 30 and 60 day sentences in county jails, and this is his first major incarceration.

Brian comes from an intact middle-class family. Both his father and mother are school teachers, his older brother is a college graduate, and his younger sister is currently in college. He has an IQ in the Superior range, but he dropped out of school in the sixth grade. For most of his life he has been a source of worry to his parents, and he has been in both outpatient and inpatient treatment. He has abused a wide variety of substances, he has never held a steady job, and he has been totally irresponsible in spite of his many promises to reform. On current examination he is charming, witty, glib, free from all anxiety and remorse, and terribly "sincere" about wanting help.

Brian is a psychopath in the Cleckley tradition. Absolutely nothing in his background accounts for his life of petty crimes and failures. He also has the psychopathic ability to charm and awaken sympathy, and his parents have spent their lives bailing him out of one scrape after another. He's not mean or vicious. Though he committed major crimes this time, they were really not typical of his habitual behavior. He's an example of primary, idiopathic psychopathy in that it's impossible to find any specific psychogenesis for the behaviors which have characterized him for all of his life.

The next man is an example of symptomatic psychopathy in that the influences on his behavior are quite apparent and the underlying motivations relatively clear. Karpman suggests that this type is more treatable than the idiopathic type.

Michael was originally sentenced to 15 years for Narcotics Violation. While incarcerated he assaulted and repeatedly stabbed another inmate, he was convicted of Assault, and he received a 10 year consecutive sentence. About the assault, he claims that he was being "pressured" and "I had to make my stand." Generally, he identified with the prison culture and the prison code, he showed no remorse for the assault or concern for his victim, and he stated frankly, "I'll do it again if I have to."

Michael is the third of four children born to his mother and two different men, all born out of wedlock, and the family subsisted primarily on welfare. Though of average intelligence, he was disruptive in school almost from the first, and he quit school as soon as he turned 16. His first arrest was at age 10 when he broke into a house to steal food stamps. Several more arrests led to 6 months in the training school when he was 15. As an adult he has one prior conviction for shoplifting. He admitted to daily use of marijuana and "some drinking," but he says he only sold heroin, never used it. He has never had steady employment or established an enduring sexual relationship. During current examination he expressed some concern for himself and worry over the direction his life was taking. He said, "I don't want to spend the rest of my life in jail." But he thought that might happen.

Using DSM-III criteria, both Brian and Michael are Antisocial Personalities because they both have long histories of delinquent and criminal behavior and significant failures along every dimension of their lives. Using an assessment of psychopathy, they are impulsive, callous, irresponsible, and guiltless. In the case of Michael, it's almost understandable that society would have produced him. In Brian's case there is no such understanding.

In spite of the differences between these two men, in spite of the differences in social learning experiences we will consistently find between the middle-class chronic criminal and the ghetto-bred chronic criminal, I feel we must deal with *all* chronic criminals as they are currently functioning, and to a large extent this means we are dealing with the essentially psychopathic personality. To distinguish between them as primary and secondary psychopaths is helpful and probably does have implication for treatment, but initially at least, we are probably dealing with a common set of psychodynamic variables. I don't mean to imply that criminality is invariably psychopathic, but I do believe it is best understood in terms of the psychopathic paradigm.

THE PSYCHOPHYSIOLOGY OF PSYCHOPATHY

Before moving on to psychodynamics, let's briefly consider biology. The literature (e.g., Elliott, 1978; Monroe, 1972) indicates that the EEGs of many psychopaths show abnormal amounts of slow-wave activity, which has been interpreted in several ways: (1) The similarity of the adult psychopath's slow-wave activity to that of a normal child suggests that psychopathy may be related to delayed cortical maturation. (2) The slow-wave activity is symptomatic of underlying cortical or sub-cortical dysfunction. (3) The slow-wave activity in psychopaths reflects low cortical arousal and a proneness to become easily bored.

Hare and Cox (1978) surveyed psychophysiological research on psychopaths, and among the consistent findings are that psychopaths differ from the norm in that there is only a small increase in electrodermal activity when the subject is anticipating an aversive stimulus; and while awaiting the delivery of an aversive stimulus, psychopaths show a much larger increase in heart rate than do others. Hare and Cox speculate on these findings in the following way:

> The psychopath's pattern of heart rate acceleration and small increases in electrodermal activity is hypothesized to reflect the operation of an active, efficient coping process, and the inhibition of fear arousal. As a result, many situations that have great emotional impact for most people would be of little consequence to the psychopath, because he is better able to attenuate aversive inputs and to inhibit anticipatory fear . . . To a certain extent, this may help to account for the psychopath's difficulty in avoiding punishment. That is, the cues that would help him to do so are "tuned out" and the mediating effects of anticipatory fear are reduced. (p. 219)

Though far from proven, I'm willing to accept that psychopaths may be biologically "different," which may help us to understand and treat their behavior. It is certain that they are immature, that they are easily bored, that they're stimulus seekers, that they miss cues from the environment, and that they are relatively insensitive to punishment. All of those traits may have a biological basis, which puts some constraints upon what may actually be "changed" by the psychotherapeutic process. However, physiology cannot account for criminal behavior. It may help to explain why psychopaths have interpersonal difficulties, but when those difficulties become criminal in nature, then we must look for other explanations.

THE PSYCHODYNAMICS OF PSYCHOPATHY

That there are a number of ways to look at psychopaths is suggested by the extensive literature on the subject, which is reviewed by Reid (1985), and which doesn't seem to lead in any definitive direction. In the context of criminal behavior, Yochelson and Samenow (1976) review ideas about psychopathy and come to the conclusion that there is a "criminal personality," a concept not unlike the "chronic criminal" of this text, which is not exactly the same as psychopathic personality. In recent years several attempts have been made to turn the psychopath into something else, particularly a "borderline" or a "narcissist," which is easy to do if we focus on one or another of the psychopathic character-istics to the exclusion of all others.

Kohut (1977), for example, described the narcissist's need for "self-objects" to help him regulate his self-esteem and feel complete, a proc-ess in which the "other" in the relationship is not only idealized and in-ternalized but is also placed at the service of the omnipotent ego; or in other words, the "other" is used and has no intrinsic value. Certainly, this theory tends to describe the psychopath's characteristic mode of in-terpersonal realationships, particularly as that mode has a manipulative quality. A particularly impressive argument for the psychopath-as-narcissist was made by Bursten (1973) who wrote:

> The manipulative personality is a type of narcissistic personality. His object choices are generally seen as extensions of himself; he cannot relate to others as separate individuals worthy of respect in their own right. He differs from other types of narcissistic personal-ities in at least three respects. He has sufficient self-object differen-tiation to be able generally to maintain ego boundaries and to use other people for his own ends. His major role of narcissistic repair consists of purging his shameful introject through contempt; in large measure this reflects anal mechanisms. His value system is such that truth is subordinated to image-building in his priorities. . . . Many people whom we currently diagnose as antisocial person-alities are largely impelled by these factors and should be called "manipulative personalities." True, it is often possible to see what advantage is gained by their particular manipulations, but it is the hallmark of manipulative personalities that they will attain their goal by manipulation rather than by other means because they are constantly engaged in the unconscious struggle to shore up their narcissistic self-image. (pp. 165–166)

Similarly, Kernberg's (1975) work on borderline personalities is often suggestive of certain psychopathic dynamics, particularly as he de-scribes the often angry and self-destructive acting out of borderlines, their ability to generate a negative countertransference reaction, and their attempts to destroy time, love, caring, and honesty in the thera-peutic relationship. Kernberg tends to describe the therapeutic en-counter as a battle in which even the apparently motivated patient seems to have more to gain by staying ill than by getting well, his de-fenses perhaps a defense against the ego-destruction of psychosis. Cer-tainly psychopathy has been described as a masked psychosis.

One can't deny both the narcissistic and borderline *features* of psychopathy, but the evidence suggests that both the Narcissistic and Borderline Personality *Disorders* are more related to psychotic conditions and major affective disorders than they are to the Antisocial Personality Disorder (Dahl, 1985; Davis & Hagop, 1986; Snyder, Pitts, & Pokorny, 1985). It has also been pointed out many times (Adler, 1986; Gallahorn, 1981; Horwitz, 1985; Phillips, 1981) that even Kohut and Kernberg so disagree with one another that one wonders if they're seeing the same kinds of phenomena in the same kinds of patients.

Just as the disparate features of psychopathy may be singled out for special attention, there was a time when one major psychodynamic was thought to be at the core of the condition: the failure to resolve the Oedipus complex. Perhaps the major work expounding this theory was Lindner's (1944) *Rebel Without A Cause*. He wrote:

> It is the thesis of the present work that the psychopath has never got beyond the pre-genital level of sexual development to the stage of object-love; that the socialized mode of sex, the reaching out and sharing, is wholly absent. As will be shown in a later section, the mechanics employed are analytic: precipitation by environmental factors causing an abrupt cessation of psychosexual development *before* the successful resolution of the Oedipal situation. (p. 6)

Unquestionably, psychopaths are manipulators, their behavior may be angry and apparently self-destructive, and very probably they are fixated at the pre-genital level of psychosexual development. The immaturity of the psychopath is something about which almost everyone will agree, and along with the immaturity there is low frustration tolerance, the demand for immediate need gratification, and aspect of the omnipotent ego. But to focus on one or another of the psychopathic characteristics is to focus too narrowly. The individual symptoms of psychopathy may be so fascinating, or psychopathic behaviors may be so irksome, that we may tend to forget that they are the manifestations of a profound disturbance. I think it is only Cleckley (1964) in *The Mask of Sanity* who captures the essence of the pathology.

> The psychopath, however perfectly he mimics man theoretically, that is to say, when he speaks of himself in words, fails altogether when he is put into the practice of actually living. His failure is so complete and so dramatic that it is difficult to see how such a failure could be achieved by anything less than a downright *madman* or by a person totally or almost totally unable to grasp emotionally the major components of meaning or feeling implicit in the thoughts he expresses or the experiences he appears to go through. (p. 406)

Cleckley apologized for his use of the word "madman," but he thought no other word quite so descriptive. And though there are important differences, the above is also suggestive of an as-if personality organization, an idea which will be discussed below. But for the moment, let's look again at Cleckley's sixteen traits of psychopathy, but this time I'll suggest that there are dynamics which go along with the behaviors and that things may not always be what they appear to be.

1. *Superficial charm and good intelligence.* Indeed, the "charm" of the psychopath is as a magic charm, for it's not necessarily based on physical beauty or charisma. I tend to feel that psychopaths project a naivete which is so childlike that it's disarming, and dyadic relationships assume the character of the protector and the protected, the forgiver and the forgiven, and the lover and the loved.

2. *Absence of delusions and other signs of irrational thinking.* In fact, the psychopath will emerge from the mental status examination with flying colors. He is not "psychotic" in any classical sense. However, I will later introduce the term "behavioral psychosis," for if the psychopath doesn't think like a madman, he certainly acts like one.

3. *Absence of nervousness or psychoneurotic manifestations.* This "lack of anxiety" is generally considered to be a major diagnostic indicator, but this "lack," in spite of the presenting clinical picture, is probably unreal. It is true that psychopaths assume a certain *belle indifference* to both their behaviors and the consequences, but this is perhaps best explained as a defense against an anxiety which threatens to overwhelm.

4. *Unreliability.* The psychopath is a role-player, and he will assume any role that gains him an advantage. He has little consistent concept of self which endures from one situation to the next, so he assumes the role that will be sure to please. He can be the repentant son or husband, the highly motivated patient, and the leader in self-help groups; or he can be the toughest kid on the block, the wheeler-dealer salesman, and the leader of the prison riot. Any role is possible, and while it has the effect of manipulation, I believe its aim is more defensive than manipulative.

5. *Untruthfulness and insincerity.* These are behaviors associated with role-playing, but again, the aim of the behavior isn't necessarily to deceive. Though a psychopath is capable of the clever lie, he is more likely to tell the improbable story and to defend it in the face of all evidence to the contrary. He deceives no one. It's his way of denying the realities he'd rather not face.

6. *Lack of remorse or shame.* Also called "lack of conscience," another prime diagnostic indicator, but another "lack" which is probably unreal. For though he plays roles, the psychopath has at least a trace of an enduring ego, and any ego consists in part of values. The psychopath is not

shamed by the things that shame *us*, but he does have values however peculiar they may be. There are some crimes which even the worst criminal will not commit, some acts which even the consumate psychopath will not perform.

7. *Inadequately motivated antisocial behavior.* The "inadequacy" of the motivation may be in the eye of the beholder. Just because the observer doesn't think the behavior makes any sense doesn't mean that the behavior doesn't make any sense. I believe that psychopaths have a will to fail, and their antisocial behavior is often an expression of that will.

8. *Poor judgment and failure to learn by experience.* This is a real failure only if we disregard the will to fail. The psychopath makes the same "mistakes" over and over again, unless they aren't "mistakes" at all but really unconscious purposiveness.

9. *Pathologic egocentricity and incapacity for love.* Here we have the main argument for psychopath-as-narcissist. Others *are* perceived to be objects who must serve the infantile ego, and the clinical picture is certainly one of narcissism. However, I think the dynamic picture is different. The narcissist demands out of feelings of entitlement, but the psychopath's demands are desperate cries for nurturance. The narcissist imbues others in his life-space with superior qualities to bolster *his* feelings of self-importance, and he becomes enraged when others can't meet his impossible expectations. The psychopath, on the other hand, far from feeling superior, feels empty, and he manipulates, uses, and demands in an attempt to fill a void that can never be filled. He wants to love. He needs to love. But he can't love.

10. *General poverty in major affective reactions.* This "inability to feel" might better be called "fear of feeling." I have often noted how psychopaths become emotionally caught up in a novel they're reading, or a television story, to the extent that they make an empathic identification with characters and situations, only to turn away from the fictions and become cold and unfeeling. The fiction is safe; the book can be closed; the television turned off. Real people and real situations are scary, for we cannot be in touch with the feelings of others unless we are in touch with ourselves. And what does the psychopath feel when he allows himself to feel? Reid (1978) has used the phrase "the sadness of the psychopath" to describe him, but I believe it goes beyond sadness, to feelings of utter desolation.

11. *Specific loss of insight.* Cleckley says, "the psychopath lacks insight to a degree seldom, if ever, found in any but the most seriously disturbed psychotic patients" (p. 383). Originally, Cleckley used this as one of his arguments for psychopathy as a masked psychosis, a notion which he later discarded and which doesn't have to be revived, for I sug-

gest that this incapacity for insight should be related to the strength of the psychopathic ego defenses. This in turn is related to the "untreatability" of psychopaths. It is the *whole* psychopathic life style that is defensive, not just one part, and one must wonder at the strength of the defenses, and then wonder at the severity of the threat.

12. *Unresponsiveness in general interpersonal situations.* In a sense, this means playing the game and making all the right moves with no appreciation of why the moves are right or even why the game is being played. The psychopath is the actor who has learned his lines for the first act, but he has never read the whole play. To this extent, he becomes an as-if personality.

13. *Fantastic and uninviting behavior with drink and sometimes without.* The abuse of alcohol and drugs is quite characteristic of psychopaths, one more mechanism through which they achieve their need to fail. But they don't have to be intoxicated to behave "fantastically." I will consider this in more detail below.

14. *Suicide rarely carried out.* That's the fact, but suicidal gestures are frequent, particularly among prisoners (see Chapter 5). These are generally histrionic behaviors, demands for further nurturance, and designed for survival rather than destruction.

15. *Sex life impersonal, trivial, and poorly integrated.* Another argument can be made for the narcissistic ego which demands adoration and is incapable of the give part in give-and-take relationships. But an unformed ego, which is sexually amorphous, explains better the psychopath's indifference to the sex object and his willingness to engage in both hetero- and homosexual relationships. Whatever the sex object, the primitive pleasure principle is in operation, and the partner's sexual satisfaction is irrelevant.

16. *Failure to follow any life plan.* Considering all of the above, it is virtually impossible for the psychopath to plan and behave in any consistent manner. In addition, the psychopathic perception of time is probably different from the norm. In Chapter 5 I will discuss the concept of egocentric time, which has "sameness" as its characteristic, and to the extent that the psychopath lives in egocentric time, there is no future, and all of life is now.

THE PSYCHOPATH RECONSIDERED

When we get through with the behavioral observations and the dynamic formulations, we have left before us a very peculiar human being. Whatever the books say, the psychopath has to be experienced to be believed. Consider the case below.

Arthur was in his mid-twenties when he was admitted to the Narcotic Addicts Treatment Program in a large state psychiatric hospital. He was on probation, having chosen to be treated rather than jailed after a "bust" for shoplifting. He had a long history of delinquent and criminal behavior, no violent offenses, and a history of heroin addiction. In spite of a pleasing appearance, average intelligence, and middle-class opportunities, he had failed at everything he had ever tried, including college, military service, and marriage. He had had treatment before, but this time he was "sincere."

All the patients in the program were housed on a locked ward which also held other court-ordered patients. It was probably the most secure ward in the hospital. The doors were double-locked and the windows covered by metal screens. But the patients in the program were permitted to leave the ward and the hospital grounds every day to go to their jobs in the community, and on weekends they had leaves to their families. They were locked in only at night, and all psychotherapy was in the evening.

One day Arthur got fed up with the program and decided he wanted out. All he had to do, of course, was walk out in the morning and keep going, but Arthur didn't do that. In the course of the day he gathered up the equipment he would need, and that night after he had been locked in, he sawed through the metal screen, fashioned a rope out of torn sheets, and escaped by lowering himself to the ground from a second story window.

When he was caught and returned to the hospital a few days later, the Director of the program naturally wanted to know why he had chosen to escape the way he had instead of simply walking away. Arthur was insulted that the Director would question his integrity. "When you put me on the work program," he said, "I gave my word that I'd come back to the hospital every night. I never break my word."

Shall we use the word "madman" to describe Arthur, who sawed through a metal screen to escape when he could as easily have walked out the door? His excuse, that he never broke his word, was simply untrue, for Arthur lied as easily as he breathed. Arthur looked like a "normal" young man, but his behavior was "mad."

One of my colleagues coined the phrase "behavioral psychosis," and I think it's apt. Typically, we attempt to account for any behavior by looking at the thoughts and feelings that produced it, and we have little trouble understanding the man who shoots his wife upon finding her in bed with a lover, or the man who is so depressed by his wife's infidelity that he shoots himself, or even the man who shoots his wife because voices coming from the television set told him she was unfaithful. Our problem is with the man who shoots his wife for what is apparently a trivial reason.

Having bounced in and out of reform school and prison for most of his life, Leroy, at the age of thirty, decided to marry and settle down. He did keep a job and "go straight" for nearly six months, his only problem his excessive drinking. One evening he came home from work and went to the refrigerator for a cold beer, and there was no beer because his wife had forgotten to replenish the supply. He didn't get angry with her. He simply went to the bedroom where he kept a gun, and then he returned to the kitchen and shot her. Then he called the police and reported what he had done. But he didn't wait for the police to arrive; he went bowling instead because his team had a league match that evening and he didn't want to let the team down.

It turned out that his wife was only wounded, not dead, and Leroy was grateful for that because he loved her so much. He had only shot her to teach her a lesson.

So much of psychopathic behavior seems incomprehensible, but in the end the behavior is probably no more incomprehensible than are the delusions and hallucinations of psychotics. Way, way outside the norm, yes, but having a logic if we choose to look for it. That essentially has been our experience with schizophrenia: delusions and hallucinations are not arbitrary; they arise out of the life history of the individual and in some way they are meaningful. So too are psychopathic behaviors.

If we believe that Arthur was motivated to escape from the treatment program he was in, then the way he went about doing it was mad. If we believe that he was motivated by a need for excitement, that the stimulation was more important than the end result, then his behavior was meaningful.

If we believe that Leroy shot his wife because she hadn't bought beer for him, then his behavior was mad. But if we believe that he could no longer tolerate the "straight" life and that he had a need to destroy it in no uncertain terms, then his behavior was meaningful.

In short, psychopathic behavior is incomprehensible only if we accept the explanation of the psychopath. It becomes comprehensible if we consider that the end result of the behavior was the probable motivation for the behavior. If, for example, a robber is more often caught that he succeeds, then he is more likely motivated to be caught than to acquire money. There would, of course, also be secondary gains. The excitement of the robbery, for example, that intense stimulation which psychopaths seem to require; or that infantile onmipotence, having someone at the mercy of a gun; and in some cases, certainly, the opportunity to express rage. Psychopaths are not all alike in every way, individual needs differ, but I suggest that the need to fail is a powerful motivating force in all of them. Cleckley touches on this dynamic.

> The persistent pattern of maladaptation at personality levels and the ostensible purposelessness of many self-damaging acts definitely suggests not only a lack of strong purpose but also a negative purpose or at least a negative drift. This sort of patient, despite all his opportunities, his intelligence, and his plain lessons of experience, seems to go out of his way to woo misfortune. . . . (H) is typical activities seem less comprehensible in terms of life-striving or of a pursuit of joy than as an unrecognized blundering toward the negations of nonexistence. (p. 435)

In general, Cleckley didn't bother much with psychodynamic formulations. Perhaps wisely. He did suggest time and again the infantile-like nature of psychopaths, and he did suggest that in many ways they were poorly formed or incomplete human beings. To see them in this way, as essentially infantile personalities, helps to explain their enduring characteristics, particularly the egocentricity and the primary process narcissism, and it also leads to some understanding of their need to fail. Think of the toddler who insists on having his own way, who escapes from his mother, say, in a large department store, and who then suddenly finds himself alone and terrified in an alien environment. The toddler feels—even if he cannot conceptualize—his real helplessness when the familiar supports of his omnipotent ego are removed. The psychopath may strive and achieve mightily until he suddenly *feels* that supports are withdrawn as he achieves, that he's expected to be as mature as he acts, and like the toddler he becomes terrified by the sense of his own helplessness. To fail, then, is to acquire supports as more competent others take over and direct his life, insist that he gets therapy, that he goes to a hospital, or that he goes to prison. The need to fail is not a need for punishment but a need to acquire structure.

However, lest I too become guilty of focusing too much on one dynamic, let me emphasize that it is the totality of ego defects which produces psychopaths. Teitelbaum (1965) puts it this way: "They reveal a conspicuous absence of mature functioning because they have never developed the ego adaptive devices necessary for experiencing a true sense of self and for establishing meaningful human relationships" (p. 134). Having a sense of their own inner barrenness, which is terrifying, they seek thrills and excitement to add meaning to their meaningless lives. They get in trouble not because they have unusually strong impulses but because they have unusually weak controls.

One can't ignore "the sadness of the psychopath." Teitelbaum (1965) says, "When the psychopathic props give way, the individual feels stripped of his defenses and responds with behavioral modes that can best be described as frantic attempts to avoid anxiety and depression" (p. 135.) Conn (1955) says of psychopaths, "In each case the patient is defending against *a specific type of anxiety, the dread of being revealed as he really is*" (p. 115). Vaillant (1975) says, "It is not that sociopaths do not feel; they feel, but fear lest they feel too much" (p. 182). Reid (1978) attempts to picture the desolation of the psychopath as follows: "One might think of a person outside on a cold, snowy night looking through a window into a warm room, seeing a family, sensing happiness, almost able to feel the warmth but realizing he can never be inside" (p. 9).

Perhaps one way to conceptualize the bleakness of the psychopathic personality is to turn to the idea of the as-if personality, which was first described by Deutsch (1941). In the last forty years a number of other people have written about the syndrome, and this literature is reviewed by Gardner and Wagner (1986). The consensus seems to be that the as-if personality has these characteristics: (1) apparent normality, which includes adaptive and socially appropriate behavior; (2) shifting identifications, which include instability of value and career interests along with the ability to imitate behaviors and attitudes of others; (3) lack of affect, or superficial and constricted affect; (4) easy substitution of one relationship for another and an inability to form deep and lasting attachments; (5) absence of social isolation, for as shallow as their relationships are, they cannot tolerate loneliness; and (6) preservation of reality testing.

The most striking difference between the two syndromes, psychopathy and as-if personality, is that the as-ifs do not act out and they are not antisocial. Also, the as-ifs are not so prone to be "behaviorally psychotic," so there's no question that we're dealing with two different syndromes. But affectively, virtually everything that can be said about the as-ifs can also be said about the psychopaths. These people go through life *as if* they were a part of it, but meaning in their lives—meaning *to* their lives—is absent. All that makes life so wonderful, its joys and its sorrows, love, sharing, care, concern, all the pain and all the tears, all the happiness and laughter, every feeling that makes us one with one another, all missing from the lives of these poor characters forever in search of a role to play. Is this what the psychopathic defense is all about? A defense against nothingness?

I tend to agree with the early, classical conception of psychopathy, that it is a profound disturbance of personality which almost invariably leads to disastrous interpersonal relationships. These disasters may include alcoholism, multiple marriages, innumerable varieties of family conflict, school failures, career failures, "shady" dealings, conning and manipulating, and a whole gamut of outrageous and inappropriate behaviors; and while the psychopath may often walk the thin edge between legal and criminal behavior, he doesn't too often seek out major crime. Because he does think and behave in unconventional ways, and because he is willing to take "foolish" gambles, he may indeed be the creator as well as the criminal. Criminal or not, honored or reviled, he is still a sad and lonely man.

PSYCHOPATHY AND CRIMINALITY

If all chronic criminals aren't psychopaths, the majority of them do display psychopathic traits, and effective treatment should be related more to personality characteristics than to criminal behavior. The actual behavior may be like the schizophrenic symptom, sometimes so fascinating we hate to leave it, but inevitably we come to recognize it as misdirection.

What we see when we look at chronic criminals are men who *cannot* survive in free society. With few exceptions they are grossly immature and inadequate men who have failed at everything they've tried, including sexual relationships, parenting, school, jobs . . . and crime. By definition, chronic criminals, recidivists, are the ones who get caught. Crime does pay if you're good at it, but chronic criminals aren't. Still, they present the facade, usually project a macho image, and brag about the crimes they've committed, the dope they've used, and the women they've had. They rarely show remorse for their crimes, rarely experience guilt, and they are likely to delight in behaviors the ordinary man finds repulsive. They make demands, they're litigious, and they're sneaky or hostile or arrogant. They run the gamut from the young "jitterbug" who defies authority at every opportunity to the old "jail-wise con" who keeps a low profile and "gets over" by scheming and manipulating. In these older men we see what the "jitterbug" will be one day: these old men are tired; they look at the prison through sad eyes, and they have some sense of the futility of their lives. For underlying all the behaviors, so deep as to be unfelt, is the fear and the despair. It's no accident that these incompetent men return again and again to prison. Manne (1967) puts it this way:

> To the outside observer, such behavior is self-defeating, but it provides the sociopath with a psychologic economy. Self-defeat is his aim. He thus removes himself from a confusing, threatening world. He reaches out for a controlled environment, such as a prison, which provides him with clear-cut, consistent rules, with unitary messages. Here he knows what to expect; everything is black and white; no shades of gray are apparent. (p. 805)

If there is indeed a will to fail, if imprisonment is a "solution" rather than a punishment, then we have some understanding as to why the attempt to treat and rehabilitate chronic criminals has been so unsuccessful, for life in the prisoner society has survival value, and it is the ambiguity of freedom which is intolerable. Any treatment which is imposed upon the prisoner society becomes absorbed and eventually becomes meaningless. Therefore, to treat chronic criminals with any hope of success, one must consider the prisoner society itself as part of a psychodynamic system, its influence powerful and pernicious, and its survival a priority of both the keepers and the kept.

4

On the Relationship of Psychotherapy to Imprisonment

Though prison populations represent a variety of personality disorders, when the most important issue is criminality, then there is a certain commonality to the total therapeutic experience. This holds true even in outpatient settings (see, for example, F. L. Carney, 1977), but it is especially apparent when the psychotherapy takes place in a prison where all the "patients" share the same environment and are subject to the same experiences, and to a large extent significant others in the patients' daily lives are also the same. That is, whatever the prior social learning experiences of the prisoner, in the prison he becomes a member of a prisoner society which is governed by its own code and mores, and which may bear scant resemblance to any society outside of the prison. In any psychotherapy we pay attention to the patient's environment, and we often assume a "cure" will take place when the patient learns how to alter or leave a pathogenic environment. We can make no such assumption when we work with prisoners, and we must work with them in what is surely one of the most ego-destructive environments ever devised by man. Halleck (1971b) says:

> Sometimes the system seems diabolically conceived to create mental illness. It does not allow offenders to find intimacy; it does not allow them to express aggression; it does not allow them to be independent, and it does not allow them to be responsible. As a matter of fact, it comes down hard on people when they begin to search for these values. (p. 403)

The Patuxent Institution was designed to minimize the antimental hygiene aspects of imprisonment (Chapter 1), especially in that the environment is safe and all programs are under the direction of mental health professionals. Patuxent is a unique prison, but when all is said and done, it is still a prison, not a psychiatric hospital. Aspects of correctional practice have always been a part of the treatment milieu, out of necessity, for Patuxent's prisoner-patients have by history demonstrated their dangerousness to society, so society's safety must be assured while the treatment is taking place. Even at a place like Patuxent the patients are forcefully reminded every day that they are prisoners: they live in cells; their doors are locked; their movements are restricted; and guards in perimeter towers are prepared to shoot them if they try to run away. All prisons are like this, no matter how humanistic its administration, and one may legitimately wonder how meaningful psychotherapy can take place in such an environment. Fink and Martin (1973) wrote:

> In our opinion, based on experience, no total program for rehabilitation of offenders can be successful unless it is under the direction and guidance of psychiatrists . . . The only thing that has come from the totalitarian dictatorship of the correctional facilities is the dehumanization of the individual and a reinforcement of the prisoners' feelings of bitterness. (p. 582)

However, I doubt that totalitarianism is alien to psychiatry. When the Contract Research Corporation (1977) studied Patuxent, the following was reported:

> The psychotherapy offered at Patuxent was found to be vitiated by the essentially custodial nature of the Institution; that is, the goal of unquestioning obedience to authority characteristic of a

custodial institution is in conflict with the goals of self-reliance and personal autonomy which psychotherapy attempts to foster. (p. v)

Even under the direction of mental health professionals, Patuxent did not lose the totalitarian flavor of a correctional institution. By definition, a maximum security prison means rigorous external controls on behavior, and considering the dangerousness of the prisoners, the appropriateness of controls is not the question; rather, one questions the rigorousness of the controls. What are acceptable limits? Given that the maintenance of the secure environment requires that prisoners be deprived of autonomy, to what extent may they still be granted some self-direction? One might expect psychiatry to establish more liberal limits than correctional administration, but that isn't necessarily true.

Milgram's (1968) classic study of obedience to authority suggests how even the best-intentioned of therapists can become a party to cruel and abusive practices in an authoritarian environment. Time and again Milgram's experimental subjects "punished" victims at the direction of an authority figure, even when they perceived that the victim was incompetent or in great pain, even under conditions of intimacy with the victim, even when they themselves were distressed by the punishment they inflicted.

> With numbing regularity good people were seen to knuckle under the demands of authority and to perform actions that were callous and severe. Men who are in everyday life responsible and decent were seduced by the trappings of authority, by the control of their perceptions, and by uncritical acceptance of the experimenter's definition of the situation, into performing harsh acts. (p. 275)

Prisoners become a part of the prisoner society. Do the therapists? We enter prison through the looking glass, and how easy to become a part of what we find! For there is order, structure, and a code that governs behavior. Watkins (1964) writes:

> The convict culture is a way incarcerated people have learned to survive both physically and mentally. It is, we believe, the most important factor for shaping behavior in the institution. It is a way of life; a design for living; a complex set of things to be done and not to be done, of things to believe and not to believe. It is ethnocentric. It is right to persons who belong to it and live by it. When a prisoner is fully enculturated, the culture is in him and he is in the culture.

Within it, he knows how to behave; outside, he moves with uncertainty. (p. 162)

As I've indicated, the psychopathic will to fail is in reality a plea for structure, and what better meets this need than the prisoner society which allows prisoners to act as if they were men when in fact they are in a position of almost total dependency? Inevitably, the therapeutic task is to wean the prisoner away from prison, but we can't do this if, by unquestionably accepting traditional correctional practices, we give credence to them. The rules and regulations which govern conduct in most prisons are designed to make life easier for prison administrators, to hold down incidents of serious riot and rebellion, and to please politicians and budget-watchers. To the extent that the prisoner society contributes to harmony within the prison, it is both tolerated and encouraged. That is, traditional correctional practice reinforces the prisoner's identity as a prisoner; it does nothing to prepare him for life in the real world. In a prison, therefore, it doesn't matter how good the educational and vocational programs may be, whether or not psychotherapy is available, not if the techniques of survival and concepts of morality are taught by the prisoner society. It makes sense to help a prisoner acquire the tools he'll need in a free society, but tools alone aren't preparation enough, not if his human values remain unchanged.

To some extent the prisoner society will always survive, always have some influence on the psychotherapeutic process, and the more repressive the prison, the more powerful that influence will be. I would go so far as to say that in the most repressive and dehumanizing prison systems psychotherapy is a total waste of time. I agree with Halleck (1971a) who wondered if it was "right" to help a prisoner adjust to an oppressive environment rather than to attack and attempt to change the environment, and he wondered "whether I behaved morally in carrying out psychotherapy in prison at all" (p.30). But given that there is some administrative climate in the prison supporting psychotherapeutic intervention, then there is a potential for successful intervention. Still, we are in the peculiar world of the prison; our psychotherapy takes place in the looking glass world.

ASPECTS OF THE PSYCHOTHERAPEUTIC PROCESS

One treats the chronic criminal as if he were a psychopathic personality even though this is not always diagnostically true. One treats behavioral phenomena which are perhaps best understood in terms of the psychopathic paradigm. The treatment of choice is group psychotherapy, for which there are any number of theoretical explanations, but the bottom line is that experientially it works best. (See, for example, Arnold & Stiles, 1972; Cox, 1976; Rappaport, 1971.)

Psychotherapy with prisoner-patients tends to have two related issues as the main focus. First, the self-concept, which may be amorphous or damaged. Second, dependency needs, which are a logical consequence of the incompetent ego's inability to fend for itself. Note: rage, aggression, violence, hostility, and all similar characteristics of criminals tend to be secondary to the main problems. The rage-hate *behaviors* which bring a man to prison are symptoms.

Certain events during the course of therapy are predictable. (See also F.L. Carney, 1976, 1978.)

Role-Playing. Role-playing constitutes the patient's characteristic mode of interpersonal relationships, which has also been called conning and manipulation. That the effect is manipulative is beyond question, but the motive might better be seen as self-defensive. That is, the patient really is incompetent, really is not capable of self-direction, really is lost in the adult world and overwhelmed by adult expectations, so he meets the expectations of the given situation and pretends to a competence he does not feel. Since he behaves in antithetical ways as he moves from role to role, he is often called insincere. However, he might be quite sincere in the role he's playing at any given moment. He can in the morning be the sincerely motivated patient in therapy, and that evening he can be just as sincere when he joins in a plot to escape. Since there is no stable self-concept, the situation dictates the behavior.

The essence of any psychotherapy inevitably is the relationship formed between therapist and patient, which must at some point become a trusting relationship, and everything in the prison environment militates against the relationship being formed. Trust, for one thing, is a two-way street, and the therapist knows from the outset that the patient is only "playing the patient game." On the other hand, the patient is aware of all the bars, locks, and guards around him, in every way he is made to feel that he is an untrustworthy human being, and the therapist is a part of the system that confines him. So several things are likely to happen.

First, the therapist must undergo testing. It is the rare patient who will try to scare the therapist away, although that does happen. More likely, the patient will require the therapist to furnish his dependency needs by supplying proof of caring, by granting special privileges or extra therapy hours. To run in fear of the patient is a rejection of the patient, and to deny his demands is also a rejection. These are tests the therapist cannot pass, for if the expected rejection doesn't occur the first time, the tests continue until the rejection is achieved. Therefore, the therapist has nothing to lose by setting limits from the very beginning.

Second, an attempt may be made to compromise the therapist, and this may be far more subtle than the first maneuver. It will often start with some discussion of "confidentiality": how far can the therapist be trusted to keep secrets. It doesn't matter that the limits of confidentiality have already been set, for the caring therapist is inveigled into the position of protecting the patient from the uncaring administration, even to the point of "covering up" for the patient. Thus, the patient demonstrates that the therapist isn't trustworthy because he's willing to violate the rules of the institution.

Third, conning and playing the game, openly expressing to both treatment and administrative staff a willingness to "buy into" the values and behaviors which they deem appropriate, acting the patient role, while simultaneously reaffirming allegiance to the prisoner society. Watkins (1964) says that "treatment people get special attention because they can provide programs that will make institutional life easier, and they can perhaps assist in earlier release through parole. The prisoner is taught to 'look good' and to learn facts, but not to change. Actually, he becomes a better-trained convict" (p. 164).

Fourth, the therapist may become incorporated, a particularly easy task for psychopaths who have no burdensome ego to get out of the way first. This maneuver may be particularly flattering to the therapist who begins to see so much of himself in his patient, and he may even believe that the introject forms a solid foundation for further ego-building. However, this maneuver has the flavor of "if you can't beat them join them," not an expression of trust at all, but a defense against trusting.

I don't believe I've exhausted the possibilities, for the psychopath, if nothing else, is inventive. It becomes necessary, therefore, for the therapist to be brutally self-honest and to remember always that the role-playing of his patients is designed to meet the expectations of the situation, and that includes meeting the needs of the therapist. The therapeutic relationship can be formed in spite of all the barriers if the therapist isn't co-opted, but it is the patient's task to co-opt him.

Perhaps the psychotherapy of no other group requires quite as much personal involvement of the therapist. Virtually all authorities on the treatment of the personality disorders agree that traditional methods are rarely successful, that the therapist cannot remain aloof from his patients, and that he must engage them in an intense and intimate relationship. Vaillant (1975) particularly speaks of the human process, indicating that from the very beginning the therapist must seize control of the relationship, must structure it and define its limitations, at the same time placing external controls on the acting out of the patient. They can't do it for themselves, so the therapist initially assumes the role of the wise parent. The therapist then goes on to help the patients overcome their fear of intimacy by demonstrating that there is nothing to fear, and he helps them to deal with their feelings by revealing his own and sharing with them a common humanity. The human process becomes the healing process.

As always, we're in the looking glass world. A classic description of the prisoner society was given by Sykes (1958), and his comments on the forms of interactions between the keepers and the kept are particularly revealing. He illustrates how custody and prisoners work together to keep the prison a relatively happy place for both sides, how there are "gentlemen's agreements" which provide for territoriality and which establish a heierarchical social structure, and while the two sides are undoubtedly enemies, there is mutual tolerance. Custody does—and must—have a place in this society, otherwise prisons would be more dangerous to custody than they are. Officers *may not* be hurt by inmates; that will surely bring reprisals. Open violations of rules will not be tolerated because that shows contempt for authority, and while prisoners may feel it, they may not express it. Prisoners must express to custody that they accept routines and schedules, and to parole boards they must express their belief in education and vocational training as rehabilitation. The surface *sham* is important.

Within the society itself there are roles to be played which Sykes and Messinger (1977) describe as follows: the *rats* or *snitchers*, who curry favor from custody and who are universally hated by inmates and used but not liked by custody; the *toughs*, who quarrel and fight easily and who are avoided because they're unpredictable; the *gorillas*, who use violence to obtain territory, and among them there may be the *wolves*, the aggressive homosexuals who use and sell boys; the *merchants*, who survive by manipulation and trickery, who sell or trade goods that are in short supply; the *weaklings*, who are crushed by the rigors of prison and who are always "crying" about their lot, and among them may be the *fags* or *punks*, the passive homosexuals who survive by selling themselves; and the *square Johns*, who ally themselves with officialdom and so are ridiculed. Sykes and Messinger say that from studies of prison life two major facts emerge:

(1) Inmates give strong verbal support to a system of values that has group cohesion or inmate solidarity as its basic theme. Directly, or indirectly, prisoners uphold the ideal of a system of social inter-

action in which individuals are bound together by ties of mutual aid, loyalty, affection, and respect, and are united firmly in their opposition to the enemy out-group. The man who exemplifies this ideal is accorded high prestige . . . (2) The actual behavior of prisoners ranges from full adherence to the norms of the inmate world to deviance of various types. These behavioral patterns, recognized and labeled by prisoners in the pungent argot of the dispossessed, form a collection of social roles which, with their interrelationships, constitute the inmate social system. (p. 188)

Dynamically, all of this feeds the role-playing needs of the inmates, who acquire not only a "prisoner" identification but also an identification within the prisoner society. What is most peculiar about this society is that there are no "decent" roles; that is, no role that prepares a man to live in a society that is not ruled by force and repression. The average prisoner learns either to submit, manipulate, or take by force in order to survive. To practice the golden rule is to court disaster; honesty is *not* the best policy; human life has no intrinsic value; one has only the rights one has strength enough to take and defend; and anyone who believes in basic human decency, caring, and justice is both a sucker and a potential victim. Anyone who survives this society and emerges from the prison still holding onto the values of the larger society must have had an exceptionally strong ego to begin with, he is not the ordinary criminal, and he is certainly not a psychopath.

One of the main therapeutic tasks, therefore, is to interfere with the role-playing and to demonstrate the fallacy of the prisoner society, which isn't easy, for the patient continues to be a prisoner while he's in treatment and his very survival depends upon some adherence to the prisoner code and to the expectations of custody. Even when the milieu is therapeutic, it is still dangerous for prisoners to express how they really feel. Expressions of aggression will certainly be punished, expressions of intimacy looked upon askance, and the really independent inmate will likely be considered a trouble-maker. So to the tendency of the average criminal to act out to avoid feeling, we add a system which punishes the expression of basic human feelings.

Acting Out. To do rather rather than to feel is a characteristic defense in all of the personality disorders, and there can be no successful therapy until the patient starts to feel.

The first rule of therapy with the acting out patient is this: bring the destructive behavior under control. Nothing else is going to happen until that is accomplished, which is probably why psychopaths are such poor candidates for outpatient therapy, because there simply aren't enough external controls to do the job. Most psychiatric hospitals aren't willing to exert sufficient controls, perhaps because civil liberties become involved, or perhaps because controls become more punishing than psychiatry is willing to accept. Prisons do tend to bring about that control, but, unhappily, it all stops there, and as soon as the external controls are removed the destructive acting out starts again. The emphasis is on *destructive*, for the acting out as such may never stop.

Aldrich (1987) suggests that it might be important to make a distinction between "acting out" and "acting up." Acting out is behavior which is a manifestation of unconscious conflict, while acting up is a manifestation of poor impulse control, "somewhat analogous to the difference between fear and anxiety: fear, like acting up, can be understood in conscious, realistic terms, but anxiety, like acting out, can only be understood in terms of the underlying unconscious conflict" (p. 403).

The theory goes on to explain acting up as a kind of superego lacuna; that is, the behavior is not determined by inner conflict but is rather a response to external expectations. Disturbed children, for example, may through their behavior express the unconscious wishes and expectations of their parents; in which case, it may be profitless to treat the child as if he were acting out (unconscious conflict) and better to treat the acting up behavior of the child while at the same time treating the parents who induced it. Similarly, if we expect criminals, who have already demonstrated poor behavioral controls, to behave in a poorly controlled way, they may try to please us.

Consequently, it becomes important to make the distinction between those behaviors which are manifestations of pathology and those which are situationally determined. The prisoner society has its expectations, and the prison itself has its own reality, and that reality is dullness, drabness, sameness, stretching on day after day, year after year. How easy then to become swallowed up, to lose the sense of even the rudimentary self, and to give up all hope! Acting up may be a defense against real threat. To dress in an unusual way, to wear a particular hat, to sport an unusual medallion, or to decorate the body with tattoos is to say this is *me*. To hustle, to "get over," to acquire contraband is to compensate for the monotony of prison life, the ingenuity and the process of subverting the system more important than any final gain. In a sense, it's hard to argue against this defense, if the alternative is to feel the weight of imprisonment. On the other hand, if the patient doesn't start to feel, he may be doomed to be a prisoner forever.

There is, thus, this interplay between the dynamic needs of the chronic criminal and the prison structure and the prisoner society. Before he ever comes to prison he is a man who feels unworthy, unloved, and abandoned, and the prison climate demonstrates that this is true in a real sense; he has avoided feeling by acting out, and the prisoner society gives him permission; and he has been incompetent in every social interaction, and the prison structure accepts him for who he is and protects him from the folly of his ways. So long as he need contend with only the reality of the prison, he need never contend with the reality of himself.

It is my thesis that the psychopath needs and demands external controls, and we feed his pathology when we are quick to supply them. Given that we must start with external controls, how many, and how long maintain them? Most prison systems do in fact have some kind of "honor system" which recognizes that some prisoners are better controlled than others, though too often this is more related to sentence than to personality characteristics, and sentence, in turn, has some presumed relationship to dangerousness. In fact, the control needs of the individual vary widely and have little to do with the sentence imposed. In virtually any prison system we'll find men with short sentences who are so out of control that they spend virtually their whole sentence on some form of administrative segregation, and we'll find long-timers who are "trustees." In most cases, if only to meet the demands of the prisoner society, to survive in the prison with some degree of comfort, some internalization of controls will take place even without therapy. However, the prison stucture is still there, still acts as a powerful reinforcer, and good behavior on the inside is far from a guarantee of good behavior on the outside. How well controls have been internalized must always be balanced against the will to fail, which is a need for the reassurance of structural support.

The Patuxent staff sometimes makes joking reference to men who have been successful on our "escape program." One such man is Marty.

Marty is a black man with a history of alcohol abuse and robberies who first got to Patuxent when he was in his early twenties. An almost classic psychopath, he played the treatment game, and after a few years he was sent out on work release; and his first day out of the Institution he disappeared. More than a year passed before he was finally picked up for "drunk in public," and he was returned to Patuxent as an escapee. In that year he had married, settled down, and gotten a good job; he had not committed crimes. So in a short while he was recommended for work release again, and on his first day out he disappeared. This time two years passed before the police finally got around to picking him up, though he had returned to his family and friends and old neighborhood. In those two years he did not commit crimes. So in a short while he was recommended for work release again, and on his first day out . . . Well, there were two or three more go-rounds. Marty never did complete his sentence because he got no time credits for the years he was on escape, and also more time was added to his sentence each time he escaped. In all probability, if he lives to be a hundred, he never will complete his sentence.

Marty is just one of several men with similar behavior patterns, and it defies logic that they didn't accept work release and parole programs so they could legitimately be in society, since apparently they weren't going to commit any more crimes anyhow. I submit, though, that they didn't *need* to commit more crimes because they had already committed the one that counted when they escaped. Even though no one considered them to be very dangerous and didn't want them very badly, they were nevertheless "wanted men," they could be picked up at any time for any reason, and that was the support they needed to *appear* successful.

The prison therapist finds himself in a peculiar position: he works with patients who demand external controls, in a system eager to be rigidly controlling, but his task is to help his patients control themselves. To do this we must get beyond the presenting behavior, given first that any dangerous behavior is brought under control. Then it's time to take a closer look at what the acting out mechanism is all about.

Vaillant (1975) has this to say:

As the sociopath matures, he is not without anxiety; but it remains invisible to many observers—including judges and psychiatrists. Why? Neither the explanation that he cannot feel it nor the more sophisticated explanation that his anxiety is defended against by the ego mechanism of acting out is entirely satisfactory. (p. 180)

Vaillant suggests two reasons why the anxiety is invisible. First, it is so intense that our empathic response blinds us to it, and "we behave as if to ask him to bear his anxiety would be too cruel, too disruptive, too sadistic, too authoritarian" (p. 180). Instead, we protect both ourselves and the patients from the pain by accepting their distortions of reality. In effect, we give them permission to be unfeeling. Second, we are blind to the anxiety because the patient has transferred it to us. "The resulting staff apprehension then makes the patient unreachable, unfeeling, incurable, and unaware that the staff anxiety that surrounds him was originally his own" (p. 181).

The psychopathic ability to induce others to feel for him is particularly dramatic. I can't count the number of times I've been "caught," the times I've gone raging to administration because of acts custody committed against *my* patients, only to find later that *my* patients were quite content that I was upset and not them. I had to learn the hard way when I began to feel bad because a man was sentenced to many, many years in prison that the man was not necessarily sharing the feeling with me. I had to learn that it was not cruel to continuously focus the patient on the reality of his situation, that he was locked behind bars, that he would probably be locked up for many years, that his girlfriend probably wasn't going to wait for him or that his wife was probably getting her sexual needs met elsewhere, that he had lost the opportunity to be a father to his children, and that that great big world outside was getting on with its business and didn't give a damn about him. It was his job to feel bad about these things, not mine.

One way or another psychopaths will avoid feeling, and one must wonder at the strength and persistence of the defensive effort. They have a sense of their inner desolation, and they are truly terrified. In the psychotherapeutic process, therefore, any uncovering must always be accompanied by support, which the patient in turn will attempt to reject or deny. The more successful the development of the therapeutic relationship, the more compelled the patient is to destroy it. And most often he does it behaviorally. He will set up situation after situation which demands punishment and rejection, and through the sheer persistence of his efforts he may drive the therapist away. For the therapist does become caught up in the conflict, he can't ignore the behavior, and to simply interpret it, even if the patient "hears," neither controls the behavior nor satisfies the punative demands of the prisoner society. The frustrated therapist may well become a punisher himself; the authoritarian environment of the prison may well seduce him.

Among the behavioral efforts to destroy the therapeutic relationship, there may be an attempt to scare the therapist away, particularly if the patient has a history of violence, if violence has been his customary way of solving problems. Of course, the therapist is aware of the history, and if he's not careful he may give the patient "permission" to act up. It would be foolish to deny the presence of an element of danger when we work with criminal patients in a prison, but how dangerous may depend as much on the therapist as the patient. Adler and Shapiro (1973) write:

Although there are situations when work with such patients presents a genuine danger for the therapist or potential therapist, the threat is more often a feeling of inner terror in the therapist derived from his own conflicts. The feeling is often projected onto his patient, adding to the patient's fear of impending loss of control. The therapist in this situation does two things: (1) he may communicate his own difficulties with his own aggression to the patient; (2) he may act in such a way that he places the patient in a bind that either leads to flight or the possibility of some violent outburst toward the therapist. (p. 549)

Lion and Pasternak (1975) suggest that these patients often attempt to induce fear into the therapist as a way of avoiding closeness, but this is an unconscious mechanism, the patient isn't aware of what he's doing, and he's often surprised when the therapist expresses fear—which is what he should do—openly admit the feeling. As always it is the human relationship, the ability of the therapist to share feelings with the patient, which leads to the therapeutic alliance, while the confidence of the therapist provides the structure the patient needs to retain control. "Fear of the patient" is as legitimate an issue for therapy as any other, and its resolution often leads to the more significant passive-dependency issues.

Countertransference. Our patients are immature and they have massive dependency needs, and a fact of prison life is that these needs are met to a large extent. The very structure of prisons, in which confined people are dependent on their keepers for the satisfaction of virtually every need, in which adult human beings are rewarded and punished in much the same way as parents reward and punish children, reinforces immature behaviors and promotes ego regression. Sargent (1974), for example, examined this ego regression in one prison, and he found it had these elements: increased dependency on authority, diffuse rage, increased susceptibility to suggestion, magical thinking, anxiety, impulsivity, and a tendency to cling to and perpetuate the restrictions originally imposed from the outside. As a consequence, many prisoners, no matter how eager they say they are for their release, suffer the pangs of separation anxiety as the day of their release approaches. Kennedy (1984) points out that prisoners are likely to attempt suicide at two specific times: when they are first incarcerated, and when they are about to be released.

So we have patients who are immature to begin with, we have a structure which encourages their regression, and we have a therapeutic technique which promotes intimacy. How easy then for the patient to cast the therapist in the role of savior, particularly as he avoids his own pain and looks for the magical solution to his problems, and how difficult a role for the therapist to resist!

The humanistic therapist is concerned by what he sees: the inequalities of justice, the overuse of punishment, and the oppression of the prison. He no longer sees his patients as "criminals"; they are, instead, distinct human beings, and he is aware that they may have suffered long before their criminal careers began. He becomes keenly aware that the public doesn't care about his patients, except that they stay locked up, that the corrections establishment pays only lip-service to treatment and rehabilitation, and that his patients are often like Lear "more sinned against than sinning." He becomes aware that he is one of the few people who really cares. It is so easy for the therapist at this point to lose sight of the treatment, to turn the whole thing into a *cause*, and to do battle with the system as represented by the prison administration or the paroling authority. Certainly, this is the course that his patients encourage as they feed his ego with their dependency and a magical belief in his omnipotence. And if the therapist does take on the role of champion, he is doomed to frustration and failure. *The system is not going to change,* but . . . Who gave the therapist a mission in the first place? This particular battleground was chosen by the patients, the patients who are willing to wallow in their dependency, while the therapist suffers the agonies of a fight he cannot win.

Here, at what is essentially the mid-point of therapy, we find those ego-regressed behaviors that Sargent described: the patients go to the therapist for everything, apparently unable to make even the simplest decisions in their lives; their moods are labile, their concentration span short, and they seem unable to persevere at anything; there may be some major acting out but certainly a lot of minor mischief as they seek discipline as both an affirmation of structure and caring; they invest their therapist with great powers, and they may become angry with him because he's not "doing enough" to cure and free them; and they stubbornly resist any changes in procedure, finding safety in sameness. The demand is for the therapist to do more and to protect more, and the frustrated therapist may be sorely tempted, but we don't promote growth when we offer protection; we have simply fallen into another trap.

I believe it is the intransigence of the system that drives so many therapists from prison work, not that "fact" that prisoners are unresponsive to treatment. We become too willing to change our focus from the individual to the system because the system is so obviously "sick," and while off on the noble quest we fail to realize that we are once again acting out for our patients, once again taking upon ourselves the burden of their depression and their anxiety. However, the quest is not in and of itself irrational. Indeed, the therapist and the healer has the *obligation* to speak out against and attempt to change the pathogenic environment wherever he finds it, but under the best of circumstances and in the most healthy of environments, our psychopathic patients will still be psychopathic. There must always be that clear distinction between the "sick" person and the "sick" society; curing the one implies no cure for the other.

The Therapeutic Alliance. The most important goal of psychotherapy is some bonding with the therapist. I deliberately avoid using the psychoanalytic concept of transference, for though the essentially "neurotic" transference does occur in some cases, it's not common in the treatment of psychopathy, nor is it necessary. Rather, the real, human therapist is the object of the relationship: he is not used to explore old relationships in new ways; he is used to explore the self and characteristic modes of interpersonal relationships for the first time. I have elsewhere (F. L. Carney, 1972) commented on the apparently innocuous and irrelevant themes which are commonplace in the group psychotherapy of criminals, suggesting that this "trivial" material provides a pathway to the unconscious. Our patients are not terribly sophisticated. They will not, for example, ever make the psychodynamic connection between their overuse of the term "motherfucker" and their own unresolved Oedipus complex. On the other hand, they don't have to. Specific insight isn't required for behavioral control and change.

It's difficult to say just how the therapeutic alliance works. I tend to call it the "trusting relationship," but that's true only in part, for there is never total trust. The secrets of the prisoner society are kept secret from the therapist too. Perhaps it's more a matter of trusting the therapist with feelings rather than facts, letting the therapist know about the doubts, fears, and hurts, sharing with him that terrifying desolation. One angry, isolated, violent criminal psychopath with whom I had worked for years with apparently no success once sent me some poems he had written, enclosed with a cover letter which said in part: "Maybe these will help you to understand what I'm all about. I guess I'm sick. But it's tragic. I'm not sick enough." This is one of the poems he wrote:

> You are the unremembered, love,
> Like swirling shades of midnight blue.
> I'll want you till I find you, love,
> And then I'll cry my hate for you.

Over the years many ex-patients—now free in the community for a long time—have kept in touch with me. Most often it's just a phone call once a year, for no particular reason, as if needing assurance that I'm still around just in case. Some ex-patients correspond with me regularly. One man wrote: "I miss group therapy. We didn't do anything but shoot the shit, but it helped." (Therapist and patient perceptions do differ.)

In fact, many therapy sessions do appear to be totally unfocused, and I've often left a group wondering, "What happened?" And in a dynamic sense very often nothing did, except that these men who didn't even know that they could feel talked about how they felt. Therapy, too, always focuses on reality; the characteristic rationalizations and justifications for behavior simply aren't accepted; and the role the patient plays in creating difficulties for himself is always pointed out. In a well-functioning group, group members simply will not allow the membership to lie—though in the prison setting the *whole* truth isn't always encouraged—and honest, real relationships are promoted. Along the way—usually more subtly than dramatically—the effect of past relationships and experiences on current functioning is talked about, and occasionally real insight is achieved. The patients do get in touch with themselves and the feelings they've run from so long, in a tentative way, expecting therapist betrayal, attempting to precipitate it, but gradually finding safety in what may be the only honest relationship they've ever had. Then there can be growth and change. However, there are limits. I'm afraid I must agree with Conn (1955) who says that psychotherapy cannot modify the intrinsic psychopathic state.

> The residual which remains after treatment must be accepted by the patient and the therapist as a basic limitation which ... is unmodifiable. The patient remains an outsider, a person who does not belong to any group and an individual who cannot fully utilize any of our cultural institutions. He must admit his inability to love and even to feel what is going on in his fellowmen. (p. 118)

The "cured" prisoner leaves the institution with magical expectations, having a sense of himself as a competent person who is able to cope with all of life's exigencies, little aware that he has achieved this competence in a highly structured and protective environment. The best that can be said of him is that he "wants" to succeed, not that he is "capable" of success. Therefore, I cannot overemphasize the importance of treatment continuing in the community. Indeed, Samenow (1984), who views criminality and its treatment somewhat differently than I do, also considers after care treatment to be crucial. The breakaway from the prisoner society can never be complete while the man is in prison; while he is in prison we can only prepare him to make that break.

Probably the single most important feature of the Patuxent program is that the parolees are supervised by psychologists and clinical social workers, there is a continuity of care from inpatient to outpatient, and therapy is terminated gradually while the patient is on parole, not while he's still in prison. Because few—if any—other prisons have that luxury, there has to be an alternative, and there is. Parole *can be* treatment, and there are community agencies that will help.

I refer to the case of Paul (Chapter 2), who was not a Patuxent parolee, and who I saw as a part of my work in a community agency. I've seen many others like him, all in group psychotherapy, and they do respond. Therapy is hardly dynamic but, as in the prison, it provides a place where the patient can say what's on his mind, where he will be heard, and where he'll be taken seriously. The temptation to return to the safety of the prisoner society is always strong, irresistible perhaps, unless there's an alternative.

CONCLUSION

In this chapter I've presented an overview of the psychotherapeutic process in a prison setting. The influence of that "peculiar" setting is pervasive, and the next chapter will deal with it further.

5
The Psychopathology of Everyday Prison Life

Certain therapeutic problems may be unique to the prison environment. In this section I shall consider just four of them, in no way implying that these are the most important or troublesome, but simply to indicate how and why the prison therapist may have to re-evaluate his usual way of thinking.

Prisons are an emotional experience, and the cold language of the social sciences isn't always able to convey it. A book of poems by John Farrell (1986), who is a prison psychologist and a poet, perhaps helps us to have a better feel for the prisoners than any scientific study. These poems are basically communications from the inmates to Dr. Farrell, communications which he later arranged in verse form. These are *Voices Behind the Wall*, and in this chapter we'll listen to some of them.

THREE HOTS AND A COT

The shrink asks me
if I like being in jail,
an' I ask him if
he's the one that's crazy.

He says I got it good here:
I hustle, run a little store,
sell sandwiches I steal from the kitchen,
buy a pint of whiskey from a guard for ten dollars
an' sell it to an inmate for twenty.
I sell reefer, keep enough for myself,
an' buy sex from punk boys.
The shrink says I got three hots an' a cot,
an' I don't have to
cook, pay rent, or make decisions.
They even tell me what clothes to wear.
The shrink reminds me
that last time I got out
I picked up this charge on work release
an' went back inside
before I even made parole.
I tell the shrink
that he's full o' shit, that jail sucks,
but to tell you the truth,
his question scares the shit outta me.
(Farrell, 1986, p. 99)

TIME

When Patuxent still operated under an indeterminate sentence law, I published an article (F. L. Carney, 1973) in which I discussed, in part, the reaction of the patients to their indeterminate sentence, and I pointed out that whether they were cooperative or uncooperative patients they universally hated it. In prison jargon "time" is equivalent to "sentence," and whether a man has been sentenced to five years or fifty, he will tell you that he simply wants to "do" his time. The indeterminate sentence was scary because there was no time to do; in effect, a significant part of that safety in structure which chronic criminals look for was missing.

"Time" as a phenomenon in psychopathology has been discussed by several theorists. Werner (1948) believed that pathological thought and primitive thought—the thought of primitive people and the thought of children—showed many of the same qualities; and one characteristic of primitive thought is its egocentricity, the relating of all events, spatial or temporal, to the self, combined with an inability to comprehend the abstract, the objective, and the general. In pathological thought, therefore, time perception is concrete, and the adjustment of personal time to world time is incomplete. Schilder (1953) said that for psychiatric patients personal time and the present time are not identical with one another, and the degree to which patients live in egocentric time may be a measure of their pathology. Lewis (1967) points out that in *all* mental disorder there is some disturbance in the conscious perception of time which can range from vague feelings of disorientation to something as severe as depersonalization. And Bettelheim (1967) suggests that autistic children stand still in time, for time is the destroyer of sameness, and change is fraught with danger.

Physical time has as its characteristic *change;* egocentric time has as its characteristics *sameness;* and prisoners tend to live in egocentric time. To a large extent this is forced upon them by the phenomenology of imprisonment, but the ordinary prisoner can make the shift from egocentric time to physical time when he gets the chance. The chronic criminal apparently can't make that shift; he has a need to live in egocentric time, and the prison meets that need. Whether first offender or chronic criminal, the phenomenological experience is the same for all, and the meaning of time, the use of time, "doing time," accounts for a variety of prisoner behaviors.

Meisenhelder (1985) suggests that the prisoner feels "encapsulated" in time. That is, he has been given a sentence—time—and just as imprisonment physically separates him from people, it also separates him from events. He is aware that life goes on, but he's not a part of it, and he can't be a part of it until he "does" his time. Time is a burden that doesn't simply pass; it must be "put in" or "pulled." Prison time is like world time in that it has a past and present; it is unlike world time in that it has no future. The "sameness" of time is reinforced by the prison routine, a series of events which occur in the same order day after day after day, in an atmosphere intolerant of creativity and innovation. Meisenhelder suggests that how a prisoner handles time is relative to his degree of socialization within the prison, or his "prisonization." In the first stage he feels frustrated and bored and he senses that time is passing slowly; then he accommodates to the prisoner society, he becomes prisonized, and he senses that time is passing quickly; and in the final stage, as the date of his release approaches and he again starts to become future-oriented, his sense of time passing slowly is more intense than ever. Possibly, the anguish of the final stage is so intense that it accounts for the often-noted fact that prisoners who are about to be released do something to get more "time," and thus a return to the comfortable stage of prisonization.

That something happens to the experiencing of time is suggested by several studies of long-term imprisonment (see below) which indicate that long-timers suffer no particular psychological distress. These prisoners accommodate to the point where they aren't concerned about prison conditions and they lose virtually all sense of a future, and their interest in the outside world is marginal at best.

VISITORS

Your visitors come down here talkin' about
how they're gettin' along with their old lady,
the way prices are goin' up on the street,
and needin' new brake shoes for their car—
things that don't mean nuttin' to you.
You're thinkin' about punk boys,
dealin' in coffee or cigarettes,
goin' to commissary,
gettin' high or gettin' over.
After you've been inside four or five years,
it's hard to even talk with your visitors.
(Farrell, 1986, p. 105)

Prisoners aren't the only ones who become "encapsulated" in time. Calkins (1970) studied the ways chronic patients in a rehabilitation hospital handled time, and these various styles were found: *Passing time,* which consists of doing something, anything, but largely not goal-directed activity. *Active waiting,* such as watching television or reading. *Doing time,* drifting behaviors, with little involvement in anything. *Making time,* which consists of goal-directed activity and usually means that staff standards have been adopted. *Filling time,* which means a compliance with staff demands but only under pressure, and behaviors tend to be opportunistic. *Killing time,* which is essentially disruptive and maladaptive behavior.

With virtually no change, the above "styles" might also describe a prison population. Meisenhelder to a large extent bases his discussion of prisoner time on these typologies, and he then advances the idea that prisoners also try to *create time:*

This refers to inmate attempts to produce an increased temporal flow by usurping, at least transiently, control over what happens *now* in the institution. In other words, the inmate strives to be able to dictate events. Because the inmate then becomes quite fully attentive to his activities, time is perceived to pass more quickly. Since time is largely experienced as the flow of events, it would follow that creating an event in the present is in a sense being able to control, or "create," time. In prison, this is most frequently accomplished by creating dramatic incidents to which others must of necessity respond. (p. 47)

Prisoners lead soap opera lives, as if meaning to existence can be achieved only through over dramatization. Ordinary events are magnified as are ordinary feelings. Love affairs are never so satisfying as when they involve a triangle; romantic love is expressed in the gushing way of romance novels; and rejection must surely lead to suicide or vengeance. Minor conflicts must become vendettas; schemes are more satisfying when staff can be corrupted; and gossip and intrigue are the daily bread of prison life. It is only when seen in this context that prison behaviors begin to make any sense at all. When there is no future, the present says it all.

Contrary to humanistic expectations, no evidence supports the theory that long sentences constitute particularly cruel punishment. Rasch (1981) studied groups of "lifers" who had been incarcerated for three, eight, and thirteen years, and he found there was no deterioration of either physical or mental health, no intellectual deterioration, and, in fact, the prisoners' attitudes toward imprisonment improved with the years. Bolton, Smith, Heskin, and Banister (1976) found that long stays in prison were associated with emotional immaturity, but no other "bad" effects. Richards (1978) and Sapsford (1978) also failed to demonstrate that long-timers suffered any particular psychological damage. Generally, when there is little or no hope for release from the prison, then accomodation to the prison and life in a futureless egocentric time may be the best defense against despair and psychosis. Therefore, it is probably unwise to take into psychotherapy prisoner-patients who do not have some possibility for release.

Every prisoner-patient is "doing time," and chronic criminals use time as a structure which can be manipulated. Thus, we hear such phrases as, "I can do this time standing on my head," or, "I'm going to beat this time." The studies of long-term imprisonment suggest that as long as there is time to "do," the prisoner can handle it and "do" it. So a "future orientation" becomes a necessary part of the psychotherapeutic process, some attempt to jar the patient out of egocentric time, to help him see that the "events" of his daily life are meaningless if they do nothing more than keep him content in the prison. It becomes the patient's task to believe in a future and to give his life direction, but as always he must first escape the grip of the prisoner society.

CHANGIN'

The math teacher helped me get my G.E.D.
an' we got friendly,
talkin' about basketball an' shit.
The guys asked me,
"How come you're gettin' friends with a roller?"
You start participatin' in therapy or counselin',
the guys ask, "You kissin' ass?"
You start takin' courses, readin',
not watchin' so much TV,
an' you're black, the guys ask
if you're a Tom.
When you start gettin' serious,
it bothers the guys who ain't serious,
an' guys that were your friends
will challenge you.
If you start changin',
you just got to lose some friends.
(Farrell, 1986, p. 18)

THE "POLITICAL PRISONER"

In the late sixties prisoners, particularly black men, made a concerted effort to blame society for their imprisonment, and that they may have murdered, raped, and robbed was secondary to their oppression. However, prison administrators tended to act as if these prisoners were somehow different. Bordenkircher (1974), a warden, became quite concerned about conspiracy which he saw all around him, and he identified the following groups as those attempting to politicize prisoners and incite them to riot: Communist Party, U.S.A., National Lawyers Guild, United Prisoners Union, The Prison Law Collective, Polar Bear Party, Venceremos, The Black Guerilla Family and Black Liberation Army, Self-Advancement Through Education (SATE), Columbus Prison Solidarity Committee, Black Nationalist Party for Self-Defense, Revolutionary Union, Mexican Mafia, Nuestra-Familia, Aryan Brotherhood, The Black Panthers, Nation of Islam (Black Muslims), Sunni Muslims, Young Lords, The Weathermen, Isabelle Auerbach Collective, Republic of New Lybia, Jewish Community, Ohio Prisoner's Labor Union, and the Symbionese Liberation Army (SLA).

There is no question that "political prisoners," as activists, presented a threat to the security of prisons and that wardens had to take affirmative actions, but there was no reason for the wardens to believe that this threat was different from any other. Brody (1974), for example, describes how prisoners are quick to take on new roles, how they were "victims of their environment" when that was the prevailing opinion, how they were "sick" when it was fashionable to be sick, and how they became "political prisoners" when society itself became revolutionary. He points out the following dynamics in the "political prisoner syndrome": rationalization, through which the prisoner can admit the criminality of his acts while at the same time blaming them on a corrupt economic system which oppresses the poor; projection, through which the prisoner can blame outside forces for his predicament; and reinforcement of the prisoner's beliefs by the upper-middle-class who feel guilty. In essence, this role that they play is little different from the other roles that they play; it still has a defensive function.

Perhaps in no setting other than prisons must a therapist be so aware of the outside forces that impinge on the therapeutic process. It is not too often that the public media become concerned about clinics and hospitals, but the public seems to have a macabre fascination with prisons, not prison reform, but rioting and rebellion and bloodshed. The "political prisoners" knew how to gain public attention, and large segments of that public were willing to believe that the oppression of these men was politically motivated. No one could deny the oppression; it was there plainly to be seen. Perhaps the public absolved itself of responsibility for prison conditions by accepting the prisoners' rationalizations. At any rate, many forces reinforced the belief of the prisoners in the role they were playing, so that if this role was dynamically no different from any other, it was more believed. Under these circumstances, how can a therapist intervene and bring some reality into the situation? As far as prison administrators are concerned, in this situation there is no room for therapists; more controls and more punishments quash rebellions. Which, in fact, they do, while ignoring the underlying discontent and setting the stage for future rebellions.

To find one's real identity is a basic goal of psychotherapy, and the emphasis is on *real*. Many of the groups Bordenkircher names have a revolutionary purpose, but some of them also have as their concern pride in race or national origin. To become a Black Muslim may not be so much becoming a black revolutionary as a black *man*. One can reinforce pride in race without also reinforcing revolutionary ideas.

The "political prisoner" epidemic seems to be over, but lately it has emerged in a new guise, "prisoner as victim." In this case, the victim of prison overcrowding, forced to endure environments even more alien to human well being than the prisons of yesterday. The Bureau of Justice

Statistics (1986) reports that on June 30, 1984 state prisons provided an average of fifty-seven square feet of living space per inmate and confined inmates to their housing units for an average of eleven hours per day. (The American Correctional Association standards are sixty square feet per single cell provided the inmate spends no more than ten hours per day there.) But BJS and a report on the research by Cox, Paulus, and McCain (1984) also indicate no direct relationship between prison overcrowding and such factors as the death rate, assault, suicides, and psychosis. That is, while prison conditions have unquestionably become more inhumane, and while we as mental health professionals have a duty to speak out against those conditions, we may still find, if we're not careful, that we're being manipulated.

In the most repressive (inhumane?) prisons, as I've suggested, psychotherapy is a waste of time. It's like performing corrective surgery on a cadaver: no matter how good the technique, the patient is just as dead after the operation as before. Given that the prison isn't "all that bad," then we confront the soap opera aspects of prison life. That is, it's a mistake to "buy into" the prisoners' perceptions of inhumane conditions, just as it was a mistake to "buy into" their perceptions of themselves as political prisoners. There is that which is real and that which is melodrama.

In the treatment of prisoners our reality and their reality blends to form a curious third reality: they say they are victims, we know they are not just victims, yet we both perceive that they are victimized. How difficult it is for both of us, but especially for them, to make that clear distinction between the internal forces that motivate them and the external forces that perpetuate their rage! How difficult to convince them that they are not simply the victims of an uncaring society when their day-by-day life inside the prison demonstrates that no one cares!

IMAGE

This ain't no pussy-assed jail.
You got to lift weights
an' be a macho man
just so somebody won't
stick a dick in you.
You got to be
a killer or a thriller,
and I don't want to be
a thriller—no punk boy—
so I act tough

and project the image
"You fuck with me
and I'll kick your ass."
But that ain't me.
I see somebody help a kid on TV,
I get tears in my eyes,
an' I put a towel
over the window in my door
'cause I don't want no one to see
when I read my Bible.
(Farrell, 1986, p. 63)

CUTTING-IT-UP

The incidence of suicide in prisons is higher than in the community at large; the incidence of self-mutilation is higher still. Toch (1975) estimates a self-mutilation rate of 7,700 per 100,000 prisoners, and he finds that the prison population at greatest risk is white or Latin, under twenty-one, single, and with a history of personal violence. The risk is greater in jails and detention centers than in penitentiaries, and self-cutting is by far the most preferred method. Bach-y-Rita and Veno (1974) studied a group of violent men in California, and they found that 50% had made some serious attempt to commit suicide, 42% had mutilated their bodies, and that the preferred method was cutting. An examination of these men indicated that the self-mutilation could be manipulative, but most often the men reported feeling low or depressed before the act, and they experienced a sense of relief after the act; they reported an agitation and a need to do *something;* and they reported no pain during the act.

Toch makes it abundantly clear that a number of psychological mechanisms are involved in the cutting behavior and that situational variables play an important role. Suicidal behavior is more prevalent in jails and detention centers, for example, but in these settings we also find prisoners who have just been apprehended and who are uncertain about their futures, and we are more likely to find the first offenders for whom the whole experience of arrest and detention may be ego-shattering. These places hold a different breed of inmate from those who end up in the penitentiaries.

In all likelihood depression is the key factor in self-mutilation in penitentiaries too. Our inmates act out, and depression most often is the feeling they won't feel; and the greater the history of violence, the greater the predisposition for violent acts against the self. Among the most violent men in prisons there is little dynamic distinction between hurting oneself and hurting someone else.

HANGIN' IT UP

You don't see us blacks
hangin' ourselves, takin' pills,
or cuttin' our wrists
like some of these white guys,
but that don't mean we don't do it.
When all this time I got
starts to kick my ass
and I really get the blues,
I think about settin' up a situation,
like a knife fight or a shoot-out
I know I couldn't win.
(Farrell, 1986, p. 57)

A history of violence is a predictor of self-mutilation; so too is age and race. Toch suggests that prison is less stressful for the black man because prison conditions aren't so very different from those he left in the ghetto. The very young, who may be serving their first long sentence, are subjected to particular pressures, especially sexual, which tend to debase even that rudimentary self-concept they do have. Certainly, that which triggers the depression is not the same in every case; the inability to handle the depression except through acting out is common.

We are in the looking glass world of the prison. Suicidal gestures here are not an unusual part of everyday life, they are nuisance behaviors to the administration, and to the prisoners often amusing and always choice gossip. In short, in the prisoner society suicidal behavior is not really a "serious" matter. Even the man who attempts it is unlikely to take it seriously. The therapist used to dealing with suicide in the outside world may find himself befuddled.

If a patient attempts to commit suicide he is motivated to die; that's the conventional logic, but it isn't necessarily the logic of the psychopath. The immediate result of cutting-it-up is a trip to the hospital, medical attention, and perhaps a chance to enjoy a clean hospital room for a few days; so that may be the objective. Where there are no therapists, the on-call psychiatrist, also known as the "candyman," will generally prescribe some pills, which also may be a goal. Where there is a therapist, he may sit at the bedside and make cooing sounds; and that's nice too. In any event, death is not the issue.

That death may not be the objective doesn't mean the depression or the rage aren't there. But the chances of reaching them or uncovering them in the immediate situation are almost nil. Because the situation is in fact life-threatening, the administration and the therapist *must* act, *must* show at least immediate concern, and once again the psychopath revels in the caring while others feel the anxiety he will not feel. Perhaps later—if there is psychotherapy in this prison—the therapist may try to delve beneath the surface, but where there is no therapy, the "candy-man" reigns supreme.

Prisons do not promote deep, abiding, and caring relationships; the death of the individual achieves insignificance. The therapist who would work in a prison must understand this. When an inmate dies, the prisoner society takes note but does not mourn. When it's death by suicide, the administration curses the additional paperwork and hopes that the news media won't make a fuss. That is the stark reality of the looking glass world.

HOMOSEXUALITY

The prevalence of abnormal sexual behavior in prisons is well known. Karpman (1954) says, "The sexual urge is too elemental to be controlled by confinement. The prisoner may first struggle to maintain heterosexuality, but opportunities for sublimation are impossible, and abnormal forms of expression are often adopted from necessity" (p. 413). Sexual deviation in men's prisons takes the form of nocturnal emissions, masturbation, and homosexuality.

WILDROOT

This cop, he asks me
if I turned fag
doin' so much time.
I told him why
I didn't turn fag.
If it started gettin' to me
I'd lock in,
take three or four hits of speed,
get my tube of Wildroot,
an' beat off for three hours.
I'll tell you, after that
you won't turn fag

but you can't
hardly walk.
(Farrell, 1986, p. 109)

Prison homosexuality is virtually a universal phenomenon. Sykes
(1958) details the various patterns of homosexual behavior in prisons,
describing the roles that are played, the rewards that come with playing
these roles, and the indifference, encouragement, or amused tolerance
of the keepers who observe the role-playing. Ibrahim (1974) felt that
prison homosexuality in the United States was tolerated by wardens and
administrators because it helped to keep peace in the prisons. Price
(1984) found that prisoners in Australia play sex roles comparable to
those in American prisons. Srivastava (1974), studying sex life in a
prison in India, concluded that the incidence of homosexuality was
lower than in Western societies because Indian society was less tolerant
of homosexual behavior. In a comprehensive study of the sexual behavior of inmates in federal prisons in the United States, Nacci and Kane
(1984) discovered that sexual assaults were relatively rare, but consenting relations between men were openly approved of by the inmates and
covertly tolerated by the guards, and that the most desirable sexual
partners were feminine-appearing and passive men; prisoners felt that
they were adapting to their situation and few of them considered themselves homosexual.

DENIAL

This guy called me a punk,
said I was takin' dick,
so I banged him in the mouth.
I ain't no homosexual.
I ain't one of them
muthafuckin' faggots.
'Sure, I have sex with men,
but I'm the pitcher
not the catcher.
(Farrell, 1986, p. 32)

From prison to prison—even from country to country—the sex role
of prisoners do not vary and they are well-defined, they have their obligations and limitations, and the roles have survival value in the prisoner
society. Most often when the public thinks of young men being placed in
the prison predicament, it thinks of its own children, and its own chil-

dren probably wouldn't survive. One must remember that the young men who ordinarily end up in prison, no matter how innocent-appearing, generally have histories of maladjustment and antisocial behavior. They aren't "normal"; they likely have that combination of ego-deficits which has already led them to play many roles, and the assumption of a homosexual role is just another parameter of their experience. Men who are in and out of prison regularly easily make the shift between homosexual and heterosexual behavior; the sex object, inside or outside of the prison, rarely is as important as the hedonistic delight in the sex act, and that which we usually call love, the caring of one person for another, is missing in either case. To be a "pretty boy" in prison, thereby receiving protection and various other benefits, is not ego-shattering, not if one has characteristically used youth and charm to manipulate others; and to be the possessor of a "pretty boy" is to have status among ones peers.

Prison homosexuality has little more meaning than this. Yes, there are occasional innocent boys who are raped and shattered by the experience, but, as with suicidal behaviors, this is more likely to occur in jails and detention centers, and in those places authorities have a particular responsibility to protect the innocent. They may have that same responsibility in penitentiaries, but in these huge places, ruled by a coalition of prisoners and guards, it is unlikely that the innocent will survive. The individual accommodates, attaining any role he can which the prisoner society will tolerate, or he escapes through suicide or psychosis. In the end the prisoner society survives.

THE RESCUE

Buck asks me to act like a gorilla
an' bogart this new boy, Bunny,
so Buck can come over,
tell me to back off,
an' it'll look like
he's rescuin' Bunny.
Buck says if he's gonna
have sex with a man,
he's not gonna do it
with one o' them six-six weight lifters;
he's gonna do it with
a guy that looks like a girl.
Buck is givin' Bunny
reefer and cheese sandwiches

he steals from the kitchen.
Bunny is young, he's scared,
an' he don't know what's goin' on.
He looks real happy
when he thinks Buck is rescuin' him,
and he's smokin' that reefer
an' eatin' them cheese sandwiches.
Bunny doesn't realize there's a price
he's got to pay.
Buck is gonna tell him,
"Look, I took care of you
when you needed it,
now it's my turn. I need."
Buck is gonna scale that fish.
(Farrell, 1986, p. 83)

In any prison we find "couples" who establish and maintain a relatively enduring relationship. They are couples for whom the human relationship has become more important than the role-playing, people
who have managed to find that opportunity which prisons are designed
to deny, the opportunity for intimacy with another human being. It may
be significant that they can do it in prison but they can't do it outside.
Maybe in prison they can find stability because they are so circum-
scribed and the prison structure is so rigid. The very range of alternatives outside of prison makes that life the more confusing and dangerous. In prison, the roles being defined for every man, one can care with
little fear of being hurt. The sexual behavior that begins as a game can
develop into a meaningful experience. Perhaps there is safety, too, in
knowing that the relationship isn't expected to last forever, that it is
meaningful only at this time and in this place.

Homosexuality is a fact of prison life, and as therapists we observe behaviors which in normal society engender anxiety and guilt and which
are here accepted as the norm. Our own values, our own morality, may
become an issue. We try to protect the innocent, but we aren't going to
find many innocents. In the long run it's probably better to avoid taking
a moral stance with regard to the sex acts and to focus on the other con-
comitants of the sexual behavior. For example, that the "punk" is willing
to sell his body says something about how he values himself; the aggressive behavior of the "wolf" says something about how he values others;
and the willing acceptance of the prison moral code says something
about them all. When there is coupling, it is important for these men to
learn that they do have a capacity for love. The therapist recognizes that

the choice of sex object can't have relevance unless there is something to choose between.

CONCLUSION

In this space I have touched upon only a few of those variables which make psychotherapy in prison so different from therapy anyplace else, and I have tried to suggest how difficult this task can be. Obviously, I believe that any successful treatment of prisoners requires a totally new corrections approach, but I'm realist enough to know that if it comes at all it is many years away. In the meantime, even within existing structure, the therapist may have more of an impact than he realizes. If nothing else, he is a caring person in this alien world where so few people care. They're prisoners, criminals, inmates . . . but if we are to touch them meaningfully at all, then we must touch their humanity.

TWENTY-ONE

Monday was my birthday
an' when I went down
to do my job washin' pots,
Mrs. Jones, the civilian employee
who runs the kitchen,
brought out a birthday cake.
I just turned around and left.
I couldn't handle it, man.
I'm twenty-one years old
and I never had a birthday cake before.
I'd just figure
another mothafuckin' year went by.
Later I told her I'm sorry,
I'm not ungrateful,
I just couldn't handle it.
(Farrell, 1986, p. 100)

6
Criminality and the Addictions

Drug and alcohol addiction are components of crime but not causes of crime. Addiction may be one of the symptoms of criminality, and to treat the sympton without regard to the totality of the disturbance may be profitless. It may also be a mistake to consider that an addiction to alcohol and an addiction to narcotics is the same thing, an *addiction,* and that the substance of choice isn't very relevant. While the recent literature (e.g., Collins, 1981; Treece & Khantzian, 1986) almost universally makes a clear distinction between addiction and criminality, there seems to be diminished interest in distinguishing between the addictions on the basis of psychodyamics. Carroll (1980) says that the personalities of alcoholics and narcotic addicts are more alike than different. "The common core which underlies *all* forms of substance abuse and addiction is a negative self-concept" (p. 234). That's true to a certain extent, and as we shall see, an inability to handle depression is also a commonality among addicts, but alcoholics and narcotic addicts tend to adopt two quite different life styles, which probably represents personality variables and which may be closely related to the substance of choice.

Thirty years ago, when psychiatry was dominated by psychoanalytic concepts, Nyswander (1959) made this comment: "Whereas dynamics of addiction formerly grouped narcotic addictions with alcoholism, pharmacological and psychological data now available warrant a clear line of demarcation between the two" (p. 617).

Reviewing the psychoanalytic literature to that date (1959), Nyswander concluded that the narcotics addict essentially adopts a passive, withdrawn life style, that drugs are as a "food" which satisfies the basic needs of hunger, sex, and freedom from anxiety and pain. "This is in marked contrast to the alcoholic who chooses a drug which releases inhibition and becomes belligerent, exhibitionistic, grandiose, etc." (p. 618).

In the same volume (*American Handbook of Psychiatry*) Zwerling and Rosenbaum (1959) summarize the psychoanalytic literature on alcoholism in this way:

> The alcoholic is seen as having been rendered vulnerable, by early security-threatening experiences of deprivation, to addiction to a magical fluid which dispels tension and depression, relieves the sense of aloneness, places an instantaneously available source of pleasure at his disposal, permits the mastery and simultaneously the expression of unmanageable hostile feelings, and has a virtually built-in and guaranteed array of sufferings and punishments which serve both to appease the conscience mechanism and to feed back stress stimuli for continuing the cyclic addictive process. (pp. 627–628)

Now, thirty years later, the *clear* distinction between the two forms of addiction has grown fuzzy, particularly as we've learned that there are probably a multitude of personality variables which enter into the addictive process. Nor are we so sure today that oral mechanisms and disinhibition are necessarily a part of the alcoholism syndrome (Crithlow, 1986), or that drug addicts aren't every bit as violent as alcoholics (Nurco, Ball, Shaffer, & Hanlon, 1985). We have also devised typologies for addicts, a recognition that a common set of behaviors doesn't necessarily share a common etiology. But when all is said and done, the *experience* of drugs still differs markedly from the *experience* of alcohol. I think no one put it quite so well as DeQuincey did in *Confessions of an English Opium-Eater*, first published in 1821, and I suspect his observations are as cogent today as they were then:

> But crude opium, I affirm peremptorily, is incapable of producing any state of body at all resembling that which is produced by

alcohol; and not in *degree* only incapable, but even in *kind:* it is not in the quantity of its effects merely, but in the quality, that it differs altogether. The pleasure given by wine is always mounting, and tending to a crisis, after which it declines: that from opium, when once generated, is stationary for eight or ten hours: the first, to borrow a technical distinction from medicine, as a case of acute—the second of chronic pleasure: the one is flame, the other a steady and equable glow. But the main distinction lies in this, that whereas wine disorders the mental faculties, opium, on the contrary (if taken in a proper manner), introduces amongst them the most exquisite order, legislation, and harmony. Wine robs a man of his self-possession: opium greatly invigorates it. Wine unsettles and clouds the judgment, and gives a preternatural brightness, and a vivid exaltation to the contempts and the admirations, the loves and the hatreds, of the drinker: opium, on the contrary, communicates serenity and equipoise to all the faculties, active or passive: and with respect to the temper and moral feelings in general, it gives simply that sort of vital warmth which is approved by the judgment, and which would probably always accompany a bodily constitution of primeval or antediluvian health.

Putting psychodynamic distinctions aside for the moment, let's look again at that *connection* between crime and substance abuse. In Chapter 1 I reported on the diagnostic characteristics of 846 men who were evaluated at Patuxent Institution between July 1, 1984 and June 30, 1986, and it was found that 689 of these men (81.44%) had a history of substance abuse or dependency, that alcohol was a problem in 37.71% of the cases, and drugs a problem in 72.58% of the cases (see Chapter 1, Table 6). These findings are consistent with the results of national surveys. The Bureau of Justice Statistics (1983a, 1983b) reports that in 1979 about one-third of all state prison inmates said they had drunk heavily just before committing the offense for which they were convicted, 20% said they drank heavily every day the entire year before entering prison, and about 16% had at some time been enrolled in an alcohol treatment program. Additionally, about one-third of the inmates were under the influence of illegal drugs when they committed their crime, more than half had used drugs the month prior to their crime, and three-fourths had used drugs during their lifetime. Barton (1974) surveyed 191,400 inmates in state correctional facilities and found that 61% had used drugs, 25% were using drugs daily prior to incarceration, 30% had used heroin, 25% were under the influence of drugs at the time of their crime, and 40% had been drinking when they committed their crime. The Guze (1976) study of 223 Missouri felons (see Chapter 1) found that 43% were definitely alcohol abusers, 11% questionable alcohol abusers, and 5% dependent on drugs. Williams and Singh (1986) sampled 2,045 adults who were not institutionalized and reached this conclusion:

> The results of the study indicate that the use of alcohol and the perceived abuse of alcohol was positively associated to five antisocial experiences, i.e., being arrested, receiving traffic citations, being threatened or shot at with a gun, being punched or beaten, and being unemployed within the last year. These relationships generally held regardless of the respondents' sex, race, age, education, or aggression predisposition. (p. 73)

Nurco, Ball, Shaffer, and Hanlon (1985) and Nurco, Ball, Shaffer, Kinlock, and Langrof (1986) report that there are about 450,000 drug addicts in the United States who commit about 50 million crimes a year, and that "studies of career criminals found that the majority of the most violent were heroin users and that most of them had high-cost heroin habits" (Nurco et al., 1985, p. 95). It was also reported that the main type of crime committed by narcotic addicts was theft, including burglary and shoplifting, and the second most frequent crime was dealing drugs. However, it was also reported that fewer than 1% of all offenses committed by addicts typically result in an arrest.

One of the few studies of female inmates (Miller, 1984) suggests that crime and drugs is not a male perogative. The sample was 9,500 male and 2,500 female inmates of state prisons from around the country, matched as to age, race, education, and socioeconomic background. It was found that while females had fewer prior convictions, they were more likely than males to be currently convicted for a drug related offense. Females tended to use heroin more than males, the sexes were roughly equivalent with respect to use of barbiturates and marijuana, and males were more likely to use alcohol, cocaine, and the hallucinogens. The most striking finding was that females were about three times more likely than males to continue drug use while in prison.

So there is little doubt that a relationship exists between crime and substance abuse. Does this relationship also exist with respect to criminality? That is, to what extent is substance abuse a part of the psychopathic paradigm? To answer the question, let's start by first considering alcoholism and narcotic addiction as separate entities.

ALCOHOL ABUSE

Reviewing the literature, Critchlow (1986) reports that many people, including parole boards and clinicians, *think* that alcohol causes crime, that alcohol acts as a disinhibitor and permits the expression of otherwise well controlled aggressive feelings. That's the popular belief. If true, it would mean that the criminal behavior was ego-dystonic even if the drinking behavior wasn't. Alcoholism, in a sense, would be a valid excuse for antisocial activity. In one study of child molesters, for example, McCaghy (1968) found that men who blamed their offending on intoxication not only took no responsibility for their deviance, they were also extremely derogatory about other child molesters who didn't have alcohol as an excuse. In another study (Richardson & Campbell, 1982) psychology students were given a case history of rape to read, and they were asked to assess responsibility under the following conditions: when both the rapist and victim were intoxicated, when neither was intoxicated, when the rapist was but the victim wasn't, and when the victim was but the rapist wasn't. The students agreed that the offender was less responsible when he was drunk, and they also agreed that the victim contributed to the rape when she was drunk. Surveying a random sample of the adult population of the United States, Sobell and Sobell (1975) found there was no real consensus about blame and punishment when alcohol was a factor in violent crimes, which suggests the popularity if not universality of the disinhibition theory. Surveying the context of alcohol consumption in a group of criminal events, Myers (1986) found "the more the merrier" seems to hold true, in that the larger the group the more moderate the consumption of alcohol and the less the likelihood of a criminal act; he also found that mixing beverages would lead to greater intoxication and a greater propensity for criminal behavior, and that the criminal act would more likely occur at the end of an evening of drinking then at the beginning; all of which lends some credence to the idea of alcohol as a disinhibitor.

There is probably a distinction between alcohol abuse and alcohol addiction, between the problem drinker and the alcoholic. However, how one defines these terms is problematic and may be a reflection more of morality than of science. One way to make the distinction is to accept the diagnostic criteria listed in the revised edition of DSM-III (DSM-III-R) published by the American Psychiatric Association (1987, pp. 167–169), which suggest that the difference between abuse and addiction is one of limited control over the substance versus no control, or a life influenced by the substance versus a life dominated by the substance. DSM-III-R lists the behavioral correlates of "severity," which possibly may also be called "symptoms." But symptoms of what, a disease called alcoholism, or some other pathology? On the other hand, does it make any difference? Bejerot (1972) states flatly that "alcoholism and other addictions are not symptoms" (p. 842), though once addicted the patient may become "pseudopsychopathic." However, I suggest it may be important to know just how "pseudo" the psychopathy may be.

It's impossible to survey a significant part of the literature on alcoholism in just one chapter, and the sheer volume of material suggests the magnitude of the problem and the concern. Generally, it may be safe to say that alcoholism exists as both a primary disease and a primary symptom. Typical of recent studies may be that of Hesselbrock, Meyer, and Keener (1985). They found that of 321 patients hospitalized for alcoholism, 23% had no additional diagnosis, 41% were diagnosed as antisocial personalities, 38% suffered from major depression, and 2% were psychotic. Diagnostic studies of alcoholism suggest these three distinct types: the primary, the antisocial, and the depressed. Some investigators (e.g., Fowler, Liskow, & Tanna, 1980; Weissman, Myers, & Harding, 1980) tend to give more weight to the role of depression, and others (Schuckit, 1983; Zucker & Gomberg, 1986) give more weight to the antisocial factor. Curiously, though Vaillant and Milofsky (1982) found a positive correlation between premorbid antisocial activity and alcoholism, they explained it away, saying that "anti-social symptoms are often a result rather than a cause of alcohol abuse" (p. 501). Antisocial behavior as a *cause* of alcoholism or a *result* of alcoholism is the question. Schuckit (1985) answers it this way: "The characteristics of men with primary ASP [Antisocial Personality Disorder] were markedly different from those of primary alcoholics, a finding consistent with the conclusion that alcoholism and ASP may be two independent disorders with some overlapping symptoms" (p. 1047).

To make these distinctions has treatment significance. Hesselbrock, Hesselbrock, and Workman-Daniels (1986) found that alcoholism developed most quickly in antisocial personalities, they were the least motivated for treatment, and successful treatment was rare. Lewis, Rice, Andeason, Clayton, and Endicott (1985) reached a similar conclusion, and added that depression combined with antisocial personality led to the highest rate of intractable alcoholism. Rounsaville, Dolinsky, Babor, and Meyer (1987) found that a major depression was a poor prognostic indicator for men but a good indicator for women; antisocial personality disorder was a poor indicator for both sexes; and primary alcoholics who had no coexistent diagnosis had the best treatment prognosis. Schuckit

(1985) found that antisocial personalities had the worst treatment outcomes.

The above is just a sampling of the recent literature, but were we to go back a few decades we'd find roughly the same thing: that the more antisocial the alcoholic, the less amenable to treatment; and the greater the role of depression, the poorer the prognosis.

To focus more closely on the distinction between primary alcoholism and the alcoholic psychopath, it's instructive to turn again to Cleckley (1964). He points out that the neurotic drinker (his term for the primary alcoholic) wants to get well even though it may not be obvious, that he retains a capacity for insight, and that even when intoxicated his behavior is not likely to be so bizarre as that of the psychopath. The aim of the neurotic drinker is to avoid facing his failures, while the goal of the psychopath is to fail. Cleckley summarizes by saying:

> It may be said that the neurotic drinker is capable of insight and wants to get well. The psychopathologic picture is more readily comprehensible in terms of cause and effect and, under favorable conditions, is perhaps reversible. The psychopath, on the other hand, despite his superficial appearance of being a normal man, shows in his whole behavior pattern deviation and disorder that seem fundamental. His real drives, when one tries to surmise them from his reactions, strike the observer as foreign to ordinary human impulse. The process, if reversible at all, is not ordinarily found to be so. Apparently there is no latent insight that can be aroused or sincere desire to become well or, rather, to become like other men. (p. 347)

If we simply look at behavior, specifically the criminal behavior of alcohol-intoxicated persons, there is no reason to make a distinction between them. Criminal acts require specific punishments, and before the law intoxication is not a valid defense. On the other hand, if we want to treat and rehabilitate these individuals, then distinction between them becomes imperative. What happens in fact is that most alcoholic probationers are required to attend Alcoholics Anonymous, virtually the only alcohol treatment program in prisons is Alcoholics Anonymous, and many, many men upon their release from prison are required to attend Alcoholics Anonymous as a condition of their parole. Implying no disrespect at all for Alcoholics Anonymous, for psychopaths it's a total waste of time. Cleckley puts it as well as anybody: "In their relations with Alcoholics Anonymous, psychopaths sometimes show at first what seems extraordinary zeal, sincerity, and promise, only to reveal after varying intervals that the whole matter was only a sort of prank or lightly taken adventure in versatile careers of self-ruin" (p. 349). However, the traditional therapies are not necessarily more effective. For example, Brandsma and Pattison (1985) reviewed thirty reports of group psychotherapy with alcoholics, and they concluded, not very hopefully, that it's better than nothing, but the failure rate with psychotherapy alone was very high.

Alcoholics Anonymous—perhaps in combination with psychotherapy—is probably the treatment of choice for primary alcoholics, whether or not they've committed a criminal act. When disinhibition is the probable cause of the criminal behavior, one may make "control of drinking behavior" the focus of treatment on the assumption that the criminal behavior is ego-dystonic. When the essential problem is criminality, alcoholism might better be seen as a component rather than a cause.

To summarize to this point: The literature suggests that about 40% of incarcerated felons have had a problem with alcohol abuse or dependence and that maybe 25% suffered some degree of intoxication at the time of their felony. The popular belief that alcohol "causes" crime in that it acts as a disinhibitor may be true in part, but with respect to chronic criminality it's probably not true; alcohol may facilitate the antisocial behavior of the chronic criminal, but psychopathy is more likely the primary dynamic. To distinguish between abuse and dependence highlights the severity of the addiction but not the severity of the problem. Studies suggest three types of alcoholics: the primary alcoholic who does not have another diagnosis, who is probably the least criminal, and who has the best prognosis; the depressed alcoholic, who is also relatively noncriminal, and whose prognosis is less hopeful; and the antisocial alcoholic, who is the most criminal, and whose prognosis is dismal. Dynamically, the antisocial alcoholic may be distinguished from the other types in that his drinking behavior is an expression of his will to fail, while the other types drink to escape their failures.

In a later section of this chapter I'll consider treatment in more detail, but for the moment let's consider narcotic addiction.

NARCOTIC ADDICTION

There are essentially three models proposed to represent the addiction process: (1) a personality theory model focusing on the ego structure; (2) a learning theory model which involves both classical and operant conditioning; and (3) a social process model which emphasizes the effect of the peer group. Each model suggests its own mode of intervention.

The Personality Theory Model: Psychoanalysts tend to concentrate on the infantile-like nature of the addict's ego. Rado (1933) speaks of the omnipotent ego which can relieve depression and bring on elation at will—through injection. Chessick (1960) relates the act of injection to oral incorporation, and he describes a person who is demanding and insatiably pleasure-seeking. Fenichel (1945) comments on the obsessive-compulsive nature of addiction and relates it to ungratified developmental needs. Savitt (1963), who sees addiction as a symptom-complex rather than as a disease entity, points out that the object relationships of addicts are all at an archaic level.

Blatt, McDonald, Sugarman, and Wilber (1984) provide a comprehensive overview of psychoanalytic theories of opiate addiction, linking theoretical expectations to empirical findings. They conclude that the analysts ascribe one of two motives to opiate addiction. (1) The regressive motive, or the search for a state of primitive, narcissistic bliss; and this is supported by the empirical research which suggests that "most addicts appear reluctant or unable to seek satisfaction in normal interpersonal relationships and instead remain aloof and independent and use the drug to induce a blissful, symbiotic, narcissistic state" (p.168). (2) The defense motive, where the defense is against feeling intense affect including anger, anxiety, and depression, or where the defense is more the containment of aggression and possible psychotic disintegration; and the empirical literature suggests that while opiate use as a defense against psychosis is rare, its use is undoubtedly linked to feelings of inadequacy and lack of self-worth.

Objective studies based on psychological test results (e.g., Gilbert & Lombardi, 1967; Panton & Brisson, 1971; Craig, 1979) tend to characterize the drug addict as follows: (1) he is essentially involved in a personality disorder characterized by antisocial patterns of behavior; (2) he tends to be more intelligent, emotionally sensitive and creative than his nondrug peers; (3) he is a social isolate and he avoids social controls; (4) he avoids stress and responsibility by psychologically running away; (5) he has a low frustration tolerance; (6) he projects blame for his shortcomings onto the "system"; (7) he does not seem to have a problem with sexual identity, but he does avoid masculine occupations which involve considerable physical and outdoor activity; (8) he has a need for affection, but he puts impossible barriers between himself and others; and (9) he seeks immediate need gratification without regard to consequences or the feelings of others. In summary, the addict is trapped in a cycle of behavior which seems to necessitate drug use: he alienates others by maintaining social distance and refusing to recognize limits, by refusing to accept responsibility, and by running away from his obligations; while at the same time he has a high need for the kind of affection which cannot be obtained in his interpersonally sterile world; drugs, therefore, become a relief from tension and a means of gratification.

The above profile of the addict is not too unlike the profile of the narcissistic personality, and, indeed, Kernberg (1975) suggests that the narcissist is particularly vulnerable to drug dependence. Wurmser (1984), relying primarily of psychoanalytic interpretations, also sees narcissism as the primary dynamic of drug addiction. More objective evidence, though, comes from the work of Craig, Verinis, and Wexler (1985). They analyzed the responses to the Millon Clinical Multiaxial Inventory of 106 alcoholics and 100 heroin addicts, and they concluded:

> We found that alcoholics and drug addicts are both alike and different in personality styles. Simple comparisons between the two groups, controlling for the effects of age, still produced significant differences between them in basic personality styles. The alcoholics scored higher in the personality style of Avoidant, Dependent Submissive, Schizotypal, Borderline and Paranoid. The drug addicts scored significantly higher in the Narcissistic personality disorder. (p. 159)

Treece and Khantzian (1986) indicate that roughly one half of all narcotic addicts are diagnosed antisocial personalities, but "such personalities can be viewed dynamically as a variant of narcissistic personality disorder" (p. 405). However, Khantzian and Treece (1985) also indicate that the diagnosis of narcotic addicts covers almost the entire range of DSM-III Axis II personality disorders, and that about 93% of addicts receive some psychiatric diagnosis; they also indicate that depression plays a role in almost two thirds of the cases.

Treece and Khantzian (1986) formulated a psychodynamic theory of drug dependence based primarily on ego psychology. They write:

> The vulnerabilities observed to characterize chronic substance abusers, and presumed also to underlie the predisposition to drug dependence, are consistent with the psychology of character disorder. To recapitulate briefly, these vulnerabilities include (1) major difficulties in tolerating affects, with an incapacity to experience gradation of feelings that enable an emotionally full existence,

appropriate anticipation of distress, and the use of affective signals in smooth coordination with defensive functions; (2) vulnerability in self-esteem associated particularly with heavy reliance on narcissistic protectiveness and incompletely integrated inner self- and object images; (3) and a range of disturbances in thinking and judgment related to rigid and immature defensive and adaptive coping capacities. The concept of a deficient capacity for self-care encompasses all of these features and refers to developmental failures in the basic processes of self-regulation, self-soothing, and a sturdy self-valuation. (p. 404)

A "deficient capacity for self-care" is very like Cleckley's concept of "self-ruin" and implies "the will to fail." With respect to narcotic addicts, therefore, it may be better to consider once again phenomonology rather than diagnosis, to note both the narcissistic and antisocial elements of the personality, but to treat within the parameters of the psychopathic paradigm. Let me be clear that I am not equating narcotic addicts in general with chronic criminals. I believe distinctions exist, which I'll discuss in a later section of this chapter, for the personality theory model doesn't really explain everything. Particularly, it does not lead to an efficacious mode of intervention, not if psychotherapy is deemed to be the only treatment needed. Narcotic addicts aren't very responsive to traditional psychotherapy. Lindesmith (1968) reports on a number of studies which indicate a relapse rate of 80% in the first year; O'Donnell (1964) and Vaillant (1966) indicate a 90% relapse rate. Craig (1979) reviewed seventy-seven empirical studies of treatment over a span of forty-one years, and he concluded that "no treatment program has been able to show a reduction in psychopathic-like traits" (p. 619). Perhaps, therefore, to look only at personality characteristics of narcotic addicts is to miss a large part of the picture.

The Learning Theory Model: The basic postulate of this model is that drug-taking behavior is learned and therefore follows learning theory expectations. The behavior begins when the individual is exposed to a combination of social and physical stimuli such that he perceives the benefits of taking drugs outweighing the risks. The psychic processes which allowed this choice are outside the scope of the model.

A model developed by Porchke (1970) is probably most nearly representative of the learning theory approach and is based on Hullian psychology. When the addict first encounters drugs his habit strength (Hs) for drug use is low on his response hierarchy. Curiosity drive competes with fear and inhibition producing an approach-avoidance conflict. If his first use yields social and physical pleasure, it is reinforced and becomes more likely to recur. As the behavior is repeated, Hs increases, making it a more frequent response, and with greater frequency physiological tolerance develops. Halting drug use at this point produces withdrawal symptoms which the addict then learns to relieve with more drugs. Drug use then acquires a powerful secondary reinforcing affect by replacing physical agony with a feeling of well-being. The addict also becomes sensitized to the internal body cues of impending withdrawal symptoms, and this stimulates him to take more drugs long before actual ill-effects are felt.

The above model suggests how the addictive process starts, and it was perhaps Wikler (1965, 1971) who first tried to explain the high relapse rate of narcotic addicts in terms of Pavlovian conditioning. The drug itself serves as the unconditioned stimulus which consistently evokes an unconditioned response from several efferent systems. Drug administration usually involves a set of complex procedures—making a contact to buy drugs, the drug culture itself, acquiring paraphernalia, preparing to "fire," and "firing up"—all of which can function as a conditioned stimulus. O'Brien, Ehrman, and Ternes (1984), commenting on conditioning experiments since Wikler, suggest at least two possible responses to the conditioning: (1) the conditioned stimuli may produce opiod-like effects, a physiological response in the absence of the drug itself; or (2) the conditioned stimuli may produce withdrawal-like effects, physiological pain long after the system is drug-free. Among the conditioned stimuli are the family, friends, and neighborhoods associated with the addiction, and most addicts return to these old neighborhoods after treatment—or prison. Thus, even in the absence of drugs, a familiar scene or a familiar face may trigger an opiod-like effect or a withdrawal-like effect, which in turn may lead to drug taking to enhance the pleasure or avoid the pain.

One implication of this model is "reconditioning" as a treatment modality, which for the most part means methadone maintainance, which over the years has not lived up to its well-touted reputation. Dupont (1972) claimed that the introduction of methadone programs dramatically decreased the crime rate in Washington, D.C., but during the period of his study the police force in that city also doubled in size. Maddux and Bowden (1972) pointed out that many addicts did not abstain from other drugs while they were on methadone, and they said that "most of the published data do not clearly demonstrate reduced criminal behavior" (p. 445). Weppner, Stephens, and Conrad (1972) suggested that addicts were as likely to use methadone illegally or inapropriately as any other drug. Anderson and Nutter (1975), studying one methadone program, found that 44% of the addicts were arrested subsequent to their admission to the program, that there was low abstinence from heroin, and that there was no improvement in employment or social condition. Nurco et al. (1986) clearly demonstrate that addicts continue criminal activity while in a methadone maintenance program. Thus, while a learning theory model contributes to an understanding of narcotic addiction, it cannot stand alone. After all, it was Pavlov himself who pointed out that a significant variable in conditioning was the temperment of the subject.

The Social Process Model: Ausubel (1961) suggests that precipitating and predisposing factors cause the "disease" of addiction. Precipitating factors are external and stem from the addict's social setting: how available are drugs to him and how will his family and community accept his drug use? Predisposing factors are essentially the internal makeup of the potential addict, and the closer he approaches the maturationally deficient prototype of the personality theorists, the more likely he will become addicted. Ausubel points out that there is a necessary relationship between the external and the internal factors. For example, if drugs simply are not available, no matter how predisposed an individual, he will never become an addict. On the other hand, when drugs are widely available, even individuals with little predisposition may become drug users and/or addicts. In ghetto areas drug use may easily be the way a youngster expresses his rebellion and finds identity with the gang, but with maturity those with little predisposition may shift to an identification with broader cultural values.

Feldman (1968) describes the ghetto as an action-oriented, risk-taking subculture where achievement is measured by ability to undertake and succeed at dangerous, difficult tasks, and he sees addiction as resulting from the high status and prestige awarded drug users. To be able to use drugs without becoming addicted, to succeed where so many members of the group have failed, is seen as a highly impressive feat which would produce great increase in status. Thus, prospective drug addicts seek out drugs not out of pathology but for upward mobility within the subculture. (Though these comments were made about the heroin users of the ghetto, one wonders if they might not also apply to the cocaine users among the well-to-do.) Separate from these status-seeking factors are those that support continued use leading to addiction. For this to occur the user must experience a positive physiological response to the drug and must learn to enjoy the effect. At this point he begins to reorganize his personal values, shifting from an action-seeking orientation to one more in harmony with his drug-induced mood. With this shift in values comes a change in peer group, and his associates become limited to those who appreciate and share his "cooler" lifestyle— other addicts.

With its emphasis on the social process, this model perhaps leads to an intervention technique like Synanon and its companions, another overrated approach, though it does have strong advocates (e.g., DeLeon, 1984). Shelly and Bassin (1965) described the basic technique used at Daytop Lodge, and O'Brien and Biase (1984) provide a historic overview of the therapeutic community movement. These programs are largely "confrontational" and require that the addict see himself as "stupid," not "sick." Kaufman (1972) looked at Reality House and found there was an 82% dropout rate in the first few months, but the relapse rate for those who completed the program was quite low. Naturally. A self-fulfilling prophecy: "We can successfully treat the addicts who can be successfully treated by us." Bale (1979) reviewed twenty-five studies of Synanon, Daytop House, Mendocino Family, and Phoenix House, and he concluded that they were so poorly designed that the reported relapse rates were worthless.

Deitch and Zweben (1984) write: "Synanon, the progenitor of the present day TCs [therapeutic communities], represented a thoroughly totalitarian approach. Most TCs today are far less insulated than Synanon was able to become, so they seldom reach the bizarre limits that Synanon ultimately displayed" (p. 37).

In so commenting these authors give voice to the concern of many mental health professionals, that something which passes for "psychotherapy" is placed in the hands of ex-addicts who are not only untrained but who also may still be characterologically impaired. The leaders of self-help groups are often charismatic; so are many psychopaths. The "therapist" who practices for the sake of his own ego is a shallow creature indeed, and one may wonder how destructive he becomes.

Synthesis: Actually, the prognostic picture isn't as grim as the preceding implies. No matter the approach taken to the treatment of narcotic addiction there are successes as well as failures, and the problem may well be that too often the patient is forced to adapt to a treatment that doesn't really address his problems. In recent years, for example, Narcotics Anonymous (NA) has become as popular as Alcoholics Anonymous (AA), it too is a particular darling of the corrections establishment, and it is equally as unsuccessful. Peyrot (1985) describes the NA approach in this way:

Unlike conventional psychotherapy-based drug treatment,

which is adjusted to the individual problems of clients, it requires the client to do the adjusting . . . the NA approach is based on the assumption that all its members have the same problem . . . In fact, a major portion of treatment activity consists of indoctrinating the client to the NA definition of his problem, with no compromise or negotiation over how the problem is defined. (p. 1514)

In fact, if the treatment is geared to the patient rather then to the theoretical set of the treater, prognosis for narcotic addicts may be even better than for alcoholics. Cohen (1982, 1985) has proposed a five-part typology for addicts and comments on implications for treatment, while some time ago Ausubel (1961) suggested a three-part typology. For purposes of discussion here, I will accept Ausubel's three categories and collapse Cohen's categories into them.

The first of Ausubel's categories is *addiction associated with neuropsychiatric disorder,* which is equivalent to Cohen's *emotionally sick addict.* Within this category we find severely neurotic and psychotic individuals, people who have a mental illness which includes drug taking as just one of the symptoms. Perhaps, in the psychodynamic model, some of these people use drugs to avoid psychotic disintegration, but whatever the motive, it is the underlying disease process that is the problem, which the addiction may exacerbate, but which freedom from drugs will not cure. Any effective treatment, therefore, must address the process, and none of the behavioral control methods do. Similarly, these people who are already ego-decompensating cannot withstand the ego-assaultive methods of therapeutic communities. The traditional psychotherapies are the treatments of choice. Even so, Cohen indicates that prognosis is generally poor.

Ausubel's second category is *reactive addiction,* which is a transitory developmental phenomenon, and which probably includes Cohen's *normal addict* and *sensation seeking addict.* Addicts in this category may be best conceptualized in terms of the social process model, which includes the whole gamut of young men and women who are exposed to a drug culture at an early age, who experiment with drugs "for adventure" or "to belong," and who then find themselves physiologically if not psychologically addicted. At one time in our culture the ghetto was the breeding ground, but currently this "drug environment" may include middle-class high schools and upwardly-mobile neighborhoods. Historically, of course, opium was never restricted to the lower classes. The urge to attain that "most exquisite order, legislation, and harmony" of the mental faculties is not socioeconomically determined, and when addiction results, it is an unplanned consequence. Criminal behavior may also be an unplanned consequence as the "habit" becomes greater than the economic means to support it. Psychopathic-like behaviors—as the need for the drug supersedes ordinary moral restraints—may also be a consequence. In the end we have essentially ordinary people who are behaving in extraordinary ways because of a substance they've introduced into their bodies, not because of a basic characterological defect. Treatment, in these cases, may very well be geared toward drug abstinence and behavioral control, and, because we start with an intact ego, therapeutic communities may be helpful, and NA may offer the perfect support group. Cohen indicates that the prognosis for these people is generally good.

The final category that Ausubel identified is called *addiction associated with maturational deficiency*, which is described as a personality disorder characterized by hedonism, narcissism, low frustration tolerance, and poor impulse control; and this seems to include Cohen's types called the *criminal addict* and the *inadequately socialized addict*. Perhaps one might conceptualize this group as falling on Axis II of DSM-III, while the neuropsychiatric group falls on Axis I. Therefore, we are dealing with all those personality disorders which make up the bulk of prison populations, particularly the antisocial personality, and when there is a long history of criminal behavior, we may indeed infer that it is criminality and not addiction which is the compelling motive. Cohen's studies, in fact, indicate that the prognosis is good for curing addiction and bad for curing criminal behavior in this group. To a certain extent, therefore, virtually any addiction treatment technique is likely to be successful so long as the essentially psychopathic character perceives an advantage to success, and any subsequent return to drugs will not as likely be a function of conditioning as a function of the will to fail. The psychopath will eagerly take methadone—especially if its free—and enjoy any game which gives him a chance to outwit his probation officer. The psychopath is the perfect resident of therapeutic communities where the whole drama of confrontation meets his histrionic needs.

The above, certainly, isn't the only way to classify narcotic addicts, but it's a useful way, particularly as it de-emphasizes the criminal part of narcotic addiction. That is, a lot of the addicts' criminal behavior occurs simply because the drugs themselves are illegal, they're exorbitantly expensive, and efforts to obtain them must be criminal. Probably the criminal activity of addicts could be cut by 90% simply by making the drugs legal, available, and inexpensive. I don't suggest that we do so. I suggest, rather, that the association between crime and drugs is a consequence of prevailing community standards of morality, not in all cases a consequence of the addict's intrinsic criminal nature. In treatment, therefore, the psychopathic-like traits of the narcotic addict criminal—the phenomonology—needs to be addressed in any event, but thereafter treatment may be geared toward the "type" of addict with whom we're dealing.

ALCOHOL, DRUGS, AND CRIMINALITY

Studies of alcoholics and narcotic addicts indicate that "types" do exist, and one of the types, usually clearly labeled as such, is the antisocial personality. Perhaps one third of all alcoholics can be so diagnosed; and one third to one half of narcotic addicts are so diagnosed. Once again, because of DSM-III's emphasis on behavior, we can't be certain that the psychodynamic picture is psychopathy. This is particularly true in the case of narcotic addiction since psychopathic-like behaviors are virtually required in order to obtain and use drugs. Therefore, unless the life history of the individual prior to addiction suggests psychopathy, it's probably unfair to assume it at the time of first arrest and conviction. With time, with repetitive criminal behavior in spite of jail and/or prison experiences, then we may reasonably assume that substance abuse and/or addiction is secondary to the problem of criminality. We can be pretty sure we have an individual who is in search of self-negation and who will achieve it, one way or another, and we can see that his substance abuse is a means to an end and not an end in itself.

Although recognizing a common dynamic pattern in both alcoholic and addicted chronic criminals, I still think the substance of choice distinguishes between them. The passive-dependent needs of the alcoholic chronic criminal are so overwhelming that I believe his prognosis for a life outside of prison is virtually hopeless; in a psychoanalytic sense, the prison is almost literally the womb he needs, and he may react with rage and violence when deprived of that womb. I don't see the narcotic addict as having a need to regress so far. Rather, he functions at some prepubertal level where the "game" is the important thing, the life of the drug culture, its irresponsibility and sexual promiscuity, the adventure and the conning, the whole "get over" existence which, like the mischievous boy, thumbs its nose at adult authority; and life in the prisoner society isn't too much different from that. I feel the addict is more reachable than the alcoholic; I feel his prognosis is better.

Perhaps to understand the distinction we need only look at the fact that alcohol is readily available and narcotics aren't, which creates a wide difference in the behaviors required to obtain the substance: walking into a bar is no adventure; making a "meet" on a street corner with secret signs and signals is. To become an alcoholic requires only passive-receptive behaviors; to become a narcotics addict requires active seeking. Admitting that some predisposition to either alcohol or narcotics may well be a function of social learning, given that there is a "menu" to choose from, one must assume that the ultimate choice is the one that best meets the individual's needs. This includes the social environment associated with the substance, and it also includes the effects of the substance itself. One pays heed to the popular language: alcohol "inflames the passions," while one takes drugs to "mellow out." So while they may both be chronic criminals with their array of psychopathic characteristics, I find alcoholics and addicts to be quite different kinds of people.

There is also a third kind of criminal substance abuser, the multi-abuser, who ingests anything and everything with little sense of preference. Curiously, he may be the most treatable simply because there is no ego involvement with a particular substance. It's first of all easier to get to the dynamic implications of his addictive behavior, and secondly, maybe because conditioning sequences are so multifaceted, it seems easier to abstain from many substances than just one.

With regard to criminal behavior, therefore, to what extent is substance abuse a part of the psychopathic paradigm? I think the answer can be found in the many studies which emphasize the role of depression in the addictive process. That is, we turn once again to the concept of the "bleakness" of the psychopathic personality, to that essential emptiness which prevents him from ever truly participating in the human experience, that "defect" which remains even after the most successful psychotherapy. The chronic criminal, should he perceive an advantage to abstinence, finds it easy to abstain while in the prisoner society, that peculiar society itself, alien to ordinary human interaction, a substitute for the substance. (Or drug taking may continue as a form of acting up, not acting out.) Once free from the prisoner society, the essentially psychopathic character must either deal with the depression or escape from it, and most likely he'll run. To the basic character defect, though, I think we should add concepts from Pavlovian conditioning, but the conditioned stimuli don't so much trigger drug taking behavior as they trigger awareness of pain and the need to escape. As always, it is the prisoner society itself which is the refuge, not the behaviors required to get there.

It may be important to look again at that distinction between "acting out" and "acting up" that was discussed in Chapter 4, for the assumption made most often is that substance abuse is acting out—the behavioral expression of unconscious conflicts—when in fact it may really be acting up—an attempt to meet the expectations of the situation. Aldrich (1987) commented that Alcoholics Anonymous may be so successful because it "communicates an expectation that the alcoholic will be able to control the impulse to drink" (p. 406), while the conventional therapies assume no such control possible until after the underlying conflicts have been resolved, which they rarely are, because the alcoholic meets that expectation that he can't control himself, drinks, and ends therapy. The addicted probationer, prisoner, and parolee is given two messages: from his AA or NA support group he gets the message that he can control himself; but he is required by authorities to attend these groups on the assumption that he can't control himself. Aldrich comments: " . . . both prison and parole reinforce society's expectations of [criminals] continued lack of controls. The consequence is almost to guarantee recidivism; the only surprise is that a few criminals actually do reform" (p. 405).

One can address the same issue in terms of external versus internal controls, in that the more the chronic criminal perceives external controls being applied, the less reason he has to control himself. Quite the contrary in fact: the more rules there are to subvert the more exciting the game. In the absence of other therapy and simply as a condition of probation or parole, enforced attendance at AA or NA, surprise urine examinations for drugs and alcohol, forced attendance at addiction education groups, are all more likely to increase rather than decrease relapse risk. By overemphasizing the role of substance abuse in criminal behavior one gives the chronic criminal permission to shift the focus from the real problem, the array of characterological defects which leads to interpersonal disasters, and the underlying feelings of hopelessness and incompetence which makes the structure of the prisoner society so tempting. By implying that the criminal cannot abstain without support, one gives him permission to fail.

AA and NA support groups are probably very important in the lives of people who not only want to abstain from a substance but who also want to abstain from crime and avoid further imprisonment. To paraphrase Cleckley, these groups help the essentially normal individual return to a desired state of normality. In fact, most treatment programs today outside of the criminal justice system rely on a variety of approaches, an explicit recognition of the multifaceted nature of addiction, and a recognition that no one treatment is likely to be all things for all men. Within corrections, though, simplistic notions of behavioral control still prevail, notions which no more effectively address the problem of addiction than they do the problem of criminal behavior. I am not implying that AA and NA have no place in the prison. Indeed, this "treatment" is often the only treatment available, it may not help but it's not going to hurt, and it may in fact be a very valuable experience for the large group of substance abusers who are basically noncriminal. Support and behavioral control groups are probably most important in jails and reformatories, in conjunction with probation for minor offenses, and possibly in conjunction with an individual's first parole experience. When criminality is the demonstrated dynamic, these programs are essentially worthless.

The road to the internalization of controls is not a smooth road. We start with fairly rigid external controls, and in the course of treatment we relax them as the individual demonstrates more and more ability to control himself. We infer that emotional awareness, cognitive awareness, and "insight" are elements of internal controls, and as they develop we look for behavioral correlates. However, when this takes place within the structure of the prison, we are aware that external controls are never sufficiently removed for there to be a fair test of internal controls, and that the "proof" will only come when the prisoner is free again. We are also aware that the treated prisoner returns to society with an exaggerated sense of his own accomplishments and almost magical expectations for the future, often so unrealistic about himself as to virtually guarantee failure. Paradoxically, therefore, at this point in time when we need most to rely on the internalization of controls, it is almost incumbent upon us to become more controlling. That is, while we believe that an internalization of controls has taken place, we recognize that these controls have not yet been subjected to severe stress, that severe stress is imminent, and that the individual will need help meeting it. If we have faith in our therapy, we should also believe that this period of particular vulnerability will be brief, not lasting beyond the first year of parole, and our methods to help the individual retain control should be based on the premise that they are temporary, that the real goal is an individual who is in control of himself. Failure to impose controls when they are needed will probably lead to relapse, but failure to eventually trust in the integrity of the individual sabotages the goals of psychotherapy.

Just as I have little use for AA and NA in the treatment of chronic criminals, I have little use for urine testing as a way of "catching" them at their misbehavior. The goal of treatment shouldn't be to "catch" anyone; the goal of treatment is an honest realtionship between patient and therapist, and that can be extended to mean an honest relationship between parolee and parole officer. The whole concept of urine testing puts the parolee in an adversarial position with his supervisor or therapist and emphasizes the nontrusting relationship. I might modify that position if the patient were a true addict, one for whom behavioral control is the real issue, but control of substance use is rarely the real issue with chronic criminals. The trusting relationship is. To feel free to admit to real feelings and failures without fear of reprisal, to be able to relate in an honest and human way to another human being, that which has been missing from their lives all their lives, is the essence of the treatment. But when the therapist becomes just another critical and possibly punative authority figure, the treatment is destroyed, and the refuge from feelings is back in the prison. In fact, knowing that a "dirty" urine means a return to prison is very often the way a man chooses to return to prison. The aim of psychopathic behavior is its end result; so it is the prison and not the "high" that is the goal.

In so commenting, I don't deny that any of the behavioral control methods have their place even in the treatment of chronic criminality. If we have learned anything about treatment, it is that a multimodal approach is generally better than a unitary approach. I simply suggest that we never lose sight of who we're treating and why.

CONCLUSION

While the criminal behavior of roughly 80% of all prisoners may be associated with substance abuse, the role that the substance plays in the behavior is hardly uniform. A distinction may be made between those abusers who are essentially caught up in an ego-dystonic life style, whose substance abuse has led to some act of a criminal nature, as opposed to those abusers who are essentially criminal, where the use and abuse of substances is merely one facet of multifaceted characterological impairment. If we consider the criminal population in its totality, including probationers and inmates of jails as well as prisons, then the first group, the addicted group, is probably the larger. If we consider only the population of prisons, then the second group, the criminal group, is probably the larger.

The addicted group may present with a variety of psychiatric problems, but true criminality is rare. Though multimodal treatment is usually best, a treatment which addresses only the addiction and behavioral control may have value. In fact, psychodynamic therapies which do not include a behavioral control component have generally failed to reduce the rate of relapse.

On the other hand, to simply treat the substance abuse of the criminal group with any expectation that this will reduce criminal behavior is absurd. Even if the use and abuse of substances were eliminated from the behavioral repertoire of the chronic criminal, he would still be a criminal. Even to imply that substance abuse is a significant part of his criminality allows him to focus on external events and gives him permission to avoid the pain of his internal environment.

To successfully treat criminality we must resist simplistic stimulus-response notions, with regard to both initiators and inhibitors of behavior. External events do not stimulate behavior; they stimulate psychodynamic processes. We'll take a closer look at this in the next chapter, on pedophilia, which also is sometimes considered to be addictive behavior.

7
Pedophilia

Sex offender treatment programs have proliferated in the last several years (Knopp, Rosenberg, & Stevenson, 1986), and the treatment of pedophiles has received particular attention. The underlying assumption seems to be that it is the sexual "appetite" that is out of control, and that though sex acts with children may be criminal by definition, the pedophile is not usually criminal by nature. There is, instead, an almost universal willingness to believe in a "sickness" model, and so the criminal justice system has a willingness to try treatments other than punishment. That's all to the good, but the "sickness" model deemphasizes too much the criminal aspects of pedophilic behavior. Given that an "appetite" is out of control, when it's satisfied by violating others, willfully and repeatedly transgressing the laws of the community, and personally chancing severe punishments and moral condemnation, then there are certainly dynamic and behavioral processes involved which transcend the mere matter of "appetite."

The Bureau of Justice Statistics (1984) reports that men who commit sexual crimes involving children are prosecuted more often than other felons, but they're imprisoned less often and with shorter sentences; probation is the more frequent sentence. That these cases are prosecuted so diligently reflects the anger of the community, but the dispositions suggest some judicial awareness that punishing the behavior isn't likely to cure it. Nonetheless, some pedophiles do go to prison, and in the prisoner society they're the lowest of the low, hated, and frequently abused both physically and sexually. Fear of prison doesn't keep them from re-offending. Their obsession and their aberrant drive are too powerful.

In many ways the behavior of the chronic pedophile fits my definition of criminality, but for the most part I don't believe they fit into the psychopathic paradigm. Rather, I see their criminal behavior as having an obsessive-compulsive quality that is psychoneurotic in nature. However, pedophiles and their treatment is not a simple issue, and in this chapter I will take a look at the problem in some detail.

THE WHAT AND THE WHO

Pedophilia is not some rare and exotic disease. To find "youth" sexually appealing is not unusual, and, in a sense, is even a part of our culture. The *New York Daily News* (Connelly, 1980) carried a story about the eroticising of children by the advertising industry, making the point that the products wouldn't sell if the public didn't approve. A story in the *St. Louis Post-Dispatch* (Newmark, 1979) states flatly, "A lot of advertising is hard-core pornography . . . Child porn starts in advertising . . . It sets up little girls as sex objects" (p. 1). In the *Chicago Tribune* (Phillips, 1981) we find a story about the proliferation of child prostitution, not only in that city but nationwide. Ditkoff (1978) reports that "about 1.2 million children ages eight through sixteen are reportedly involved in sex for sale, prostitution and pornography" (p. 30). The commercial exploitation of children is only the tip of the iceberg, for in recent years the reported incidence of child molestation has risen dramatically. Finkelhor (1987) reports that 123,000 cases of child sexual abuse were reported in 1985, up from 7,559 reported in 1976, and he goes on to say that it is well known that only a small proportion of all occurring incidents get reported. While men are unquestionably the major offenders, Finkelhor reports that women are the perpetrators in 5% of the abuses involving girls and about 20% of boy-abuse cases. So to be sexually attracted to young people is not unusual. It starts to become unusual, pathological, and criminal as the sexualized child grows younger.

It's probably not unfair to say that psychiatry still has more questions about the paraphilias than answers. For years they were considered to be part of a condition called "sexual psychopathy," but that led to a disturbing question: Was the individual really psychopathic if he had deviant fantasies but never acted them out? The eventual resolution of the question, I suppose, was elimination of "sexual psychopathy" from the psychiatric nosology. But, currently, psychiatry has posed a very similar question. DSM-III (American Psychiatric Association [APA], 1980) will support a diagnosis of sexual disorder if the deviant fantasy is persistent even though it's never acted upon, while the revision, DSM-III-R (APA, 1987), states flatly, "The diagnosis is made only if the person has acted on these urges, or is markedly distressed by them" (p. 279). Also, just how a paraphilia is defined seems to change with the years. According to Karpman (1957), paraphilias are "forms of sexual activity which run counter to accepted social behavior and are characterized by the absence of a biological aim" (p. 596). Though DSM-III hasn't thrown that out entirely in its definition of paraphilia, it does tend to focus more on acts involving "suffering and humiliation" and "nonconsenting partners" (p. 266). Even so—curiously—dynamic psychiatry treats rape as a paraphilia and DSM-III doesn't. If there is some confusion about definitions, there is even less agreement about dynamics.

The above is to indicate that when we talk about pedophiles, just because we're using the same words doesn't necessarily mean we're talking about the same thing, certainly not with respect to our understanding of dynamic processes, and sometimes not even with regard to behavioral observations. To use phrases like "child sexual molestation," "child molester," and "sexually abused child," though we may think we're speaking a common language, may ultimately be meaningless unless we specifically define the words. "Child," for example, can probably be defined at least three ways: biologically, socioculturally, and legally. Biologically, we might all agree that any individual below the age of puberty is a child, but how long after puberty does that person remain a child? Legally, a child may be as much a child at age seventeen as at age seven in spite of his biological growth. Socioculturally, nearly everyone will agree that lower class children are far less protected than middle and upper class children and that, comparatively, they lose their naivete at a younger age. Children don't form a homogeneous group and neither do child molesters. Thus, the legal charge may be the same—child sexual abuse—but are we looking at the same man and the same dynamics when the victim is seven as when the victim is seventeen? We might all agree that there's something abnormal about being sexually attracted to a seven-year-old, but how abnormal is it for an adult to be sexually attracted to a seventeen-year-old?

Unfortunately, until very recently words and terms have not been defined with any precision, so that the literature on child sexual abuse is often contradictory, particularly with regard to the effects the experience has on the child. There are two camps, both extreme in their view, and neither very convincing. The first view holds that children are never harmed by having consensual sexual relations with adults; the second view holds that children can never give consent and that they are always harmed. I want to consider this in more detail because I think it gives us some insight into the dynamics of the offender.

What evidence is there that children are damaged by having sexual relations with adults? According to Brongersma (1984), none. He reviewed dozens of European studies and concluded, "There is no proof whatsoever that children who have consensual sexual relations with adults suffer any lasting damage from the sexual experience itself. *If* there is any damage that these children suffer, it is always secondary, caused by the reactions of upset parents on discovery of the facts, or caused by police examinations" (p. 82). He goes so far as to infer that sex with children is an overblown emotional issue, made more complex by inconsistent and often ludicrous attitudes of both law and psychiatry, and possibly the only thing wrong with having sex with a consenting child is that it violates some arbitrary standard of public morality.

That's an extreme view, but even the well-respected child advocates Bender and Blau (1937) failed to demonstrate that children *must* be hurt by sexual relations with adults. Their subjects were sixteen children ages five to twelve who were referred to Belevue Hospital after a sexual assault. They write, "The most remarkable feature presented by these children who have experienced sexual relations with adults was that they showed less evidence of fear, anxiety, guilt or psychic trauma than might be expected. On the contrary, they more frequently exhibited either a frank, objective attitude, or they were bold, flaunting and even brazen about the situation" (p. 510). Bender and Blau went on to say that these children were usually willing "victims" and that in some cases they instigated the relationship. The people who were really having psychiatric problems were the parents.

In a survey of the long-term effects of early sexual experiences, Constantine (1981) reviewed thirty studies involving 2500 subjects over a span of fifteen to forty years, and he concluded there is no universal finding that sexual experiences are harmful to children. Twenty of the studies reported that some of the subjects reported no ill effects; thirteen of the studies reported that the majority of the subjects suffered no harm; and six of the studies reported that some of the subjects even benefited from the experience.

However, those who claim "no ill effects" are careful to emphasize that it must be a consensual relationship with absolutely no force involved. Finkelhor (1979) and Abel, Becker, and Cunningham-Rathner (1984) reply that a child can't give such consent because of his inexperience and lack of knowledge. They also point out that children are in the habit of obeying adults, trusting adults, believing adults, so "consent" has different implications when it refers to a child acceding to the wishes of a grownup, and therefore all sexual acts with children must involve coercion.

The view that children are *always* traumatized by sexual activity with adults is the more popular view, even though the proponents of this view have to admit that the data don't support the hypothesis. What the data does suggest is a middle ground, that the child's perception of and reaction to the experience is dependent upon an interplay of variables. Browne and Finkelhor (1986) provide us with a recent comprehensive review of the research, warning that the conclusions reached must be tempered because terms have been defined imprecisely and research design is often faulty. To handle some of the problem, they limited their review to empirical studies of female, nonincestuous victims, and they concluded that in the immediate aftermath of child abuse from 20% to 40% of abused children seen by clinicians manifest pathological disturbance, but when victims are later studied as adults, less than 20% evidence serious psychopathology. Some of the factors influencing the child's perception of the experience are as follows:

1. Duration and frequency of abuse. "Although many clinicians take for granted that the longer an experience goes on, the more traumatic it is, this conclusion is not clearly supported by the available studies" (p. 72). Some studies, in fact, indicated a reverse association: the longer the relationship, the less the trauma. It was also pointed out that duration was closely related to other aspects of the abuse experience.

2. Relationship to the offender. The findings here support the hypothesis that the closer the emotional relationship to the offender before the offense, the greater the trauma. Studies consistently report that the most traumatic experience involves father figures.

3. Type of sexual act. The evidence is more suggestive than conclusive, but generally, "molestation involving more intimate contact is more traumatic than less intimate contact" (p. 73). Actual penetration is felt to be the most traumatizing.

4. Force and aggression. Surprisingly, the evidence doesn't support the conclusion that the more the force the greater the trauma. A possible hypothesis is that victims of forced abuse can clearly blame the abuser and so can clearly absolve themselves of any responsibility.

5. Age at onset. Some people feel that younger children are more vulnerable to trauma because of their impressionability, while others feel that their naivete may protect them from some of the negative effects. The evidence doesn't clearly support either hypothesis. "Studies tend to show little clear relation between age of onset and trauma, especially when they control for other factors" (p. 74). Age is part of a complex interaction, particularly with respect to relationship to the offender.

6. Sex of offender. There are very few studies of female sex offenders, but, generally, the experience is seen to be more traumatizing when the offender is male.

7. Adolescent and adult perpetrators. There is agreement that experiences with adolescent perpetrators are less traumatic than with adult.

8. Telling or not telling. "There is a general clinical assumption that children who feel compelled to keep the abuse a secret in the aftermath suffer greater psychic distress as a result. However, studies have not confirmed this theory" (p. 75). Generally, it was felt that this factor was also too related to other factors for its effect to be clearly seen.

9. Parental reaction. There are only two studies. Both indicated that negative parental reactions aggravated trauma in sexually abused children.

10. Institutional response. There is essentially no research in this area.

Let me emphasize that these findings are with regard to female, nonincestuous victims. For a long time it was felt that boys weren't so at risk as girls because the reported incidence of boy-molestation was so low, and while it's becoming clear that that isn't so, there have consequently been very few studies of boy victims. One of these studies (Showers et al., 1983) reports that 13% (N = 81) of child victims of sexual assault seen in a general hospital over a three-year period were boys; their mean age was 7.89 years with a range from eight months to 17 years; 38% were the victims of chronic molestation, usually by a family member; 3% were abused by females; but the study didn't assess trauma other than physical trauma. Ingram (1981), who counseled boy victims, reported that his patients were not terribly disturbed by the experience: "The emotional and behavioral problems in the boys whom I have counseled reveal themselves to be more related to the disturbance and neglect experienced in their homes than to their sexual experiences with men" (p. 186). The only report in the literature on father-son incest is by Dixon, Arnold, and Colestro (1978), the number of cases reported is too small to permit generalization, but the authors suggest that this is an underreported problem. However, incest in general is probably different from pedophilia, for studies (e.g, Gelinas, 1983; Parker & Parker, 1986) universally demonstrate that this is the most traumatizing of all sexual experiences for the child.

To me, the first thing that these studies of victims suggest is that there is probably a psychodynamic distinction between pedophilia and incest. (See also Langevin, 1983.) The distress of the incest victim is too clear and powerful to be ignored, which suggests the power-dominance motivation of the offender. Victim distress is not so clear otherwise—and may in fact be absent—and so leads to the speculation that power-dominance, if a motivation of pedophilia at all, plays a secondary role. I'm leading up to a view of pedophilia which has implication for treatment, but before we get to theory, let's first define pedophilia using DSM-III (APA, 1980) criteria: "The act or fantasy of engaging in sexual activity with prepubertal children as a repeatedly preferred or exclusive method of achieving sexual excitement" (p. 271). The emphasis is on prepubertal but I think early adolescence should be included. I also believe the problem is somewhat different when the attraction is to late adolescents even if there is a wide disparity in age. DSM-III also doesn't make a distinction between pedophilia and incest, but for the moment I would like to consider incest as a separate problem.

The Incest Offender

Hammer and Glueck (1957) call the incest offender the "sickest" of pedophiles. They write:

> For the pathologically inhibited individual, there is only one sex object less threatening than children, with whom to establish the degree of emotional contact which cannot be divorced from the sex act proper. And that is a child within one's own family, particularly one's own offspring. In support of this theoretical view, the writers' findings show that the incest group suffers the most incapacitating fear of interpersonal relations. (p. 339)

Selby, Calhoun, Jones and Matthews (1980) studied families in which father-daughter incest had been reported, and they found that on the average the fathers were middle aged and they had limited education; the daughters were usually passive, quiet, dependent girls; and the incestuous relationship usually covered a span of years. In these families the mothers were generally submissive and they "chose not to see" even obvious evidence of incest; the whole family climate provided the milieu for incest.

As noted above, incest victims appear to be the most traumatized of all sexually molested children. Finkelhor and Browne (1985) provided a conceptualization of why this might be so, in that among the psychic traumas they list is the victim's sense of "betrayal," and certainly that betrayal is the more severe the more the initial trust. They also note that after the experience of betrayal there may be intense anger, which in later life may manifest itself as an aversion to intimate relationships. However, it may also manifest itself more directly, in that it's not uncommon for the adolescent girl, after years of submitting to the relationship, to "tell on" her father.

Parker and Parker (1986) say that there is general agreement in the literature on several points:

1) perpetrators are overwhelmingly male, while victims are mainly female; 2) parental deprivation in the perpetrators's family of origin has led to his low self-esteem and massive social inadequacy; 3) perpetrators generally do not suffer from serious psychopathology or mental retardation; 4) intrafamilial child sexual abuse is generally not accompanied by physical abuse; 5) stepfathers or other father surrogates are overrepresented among abusers. (p. 533)

Parker and Parker go on to say that their own research suggests that there is a combination of two basic factors which create a high risk situation for incest to occur: (1) deficits in the father's own early parental attachment, and (2) lack of involvement in the early care and socialization of his daughter. That is, the father's own lack of experience with parental bonding makes it difficult for bonding to occur even when there is opportunity for infant care, and when that opportunity doesn't exist, either through choice or circumstance, the biosocial bonding which includes the incest taboo probably will not occur.

All in all, the various studies suggest that the power-dominance motivation is greater in incest than in pedophilia in that the sexual activity is likely to be forced in spite of mounting evidence of the child's resistance, the perpetrator uses rather than loves the child, and the perpetrator may exhibit significant personality maladjustment outside of the incest situation. This is not to imply that power-dominance doesn't play a role in pedophilia, but the role is less clear, force is usually avoided, and signs of victim distress generally end the seduction. Pedophiles fool themselves into believing that there is "mutuality" and "consent," and there is an attempt, however inappropriate, to meet the needs of the child, while incest offenders pervert the natural affection of their children to meet selfish needs. In either case, unquestionably, the child is used, but the distinction may be between child as love object (pedophilia) and child as love substitute (incest). In short, the pedophile tends to put a greater value on the child than the incest offender, and if the child does indeed perceive that she (he) is valued as well as used, this may help to explain why the victims of pedophiles tend to be less traumatized than the victims of incest.

Unlike pedophilia, incest also tends to be a family "crime." I don't mean by that that the mothers of the victims or other children in the family are willing—or even knowing—participants, but there is often something about family dynamics which allows the incest to occur and continue. There are mothers who "will not see," but there are also daughters and siblings who "will not tell" because the telling is somehow more frightening than the deed. Usually, when we take a close look at these families, we find that the psychopathology of the perpetrator has had a pervasive influence, and the family is dysfunctional even without the incest, but the psychopathology of the incest offender is more insidious than obvious, for in most aspects of his life he may appear to be a "normal" man. Generally, he is not a criminal. Rather, he will more likely be seen as too conforming, a passive mechanism which helps him to deal with inadequacies by avoiding confrontations. He is not basically an immoral man. He may need alcohol to trigger his impulse to commit incest, and his acts, until he finds the perfect rationalization, may be accompanied by guilt. But then the acts so feed his narcissistic needs that they become self-perpetuating.

The typical findings make a point of the father's low self-esteem and feelings of inadequacy, and I suggest that on the other side of the coin are his thwarted feelings of entitlement and his need to be admired. In the normal course of events most little girls extravagantly love and admire their fathers, but the normal isn't enough for the potential incest offender whose need grows even as it's fed, who sexualizes the relationship in a desperate attempt to feel like a whole man. Let there be no mistake: incest is a selfish crime; the welfare of the child is absolutely secondary to the needs of the man; the child is a sacrifice to the ego.

The following case may serve as an example.

Ed is a 40 year old white man who is serving a 10 year sentence for child sexual abuse. He began having sexual intercourse with his daughter Sandy when she was 12 years old, and the relationship continued until she was 15. At that time she told her father that she wanted to stop, and Ed stopped. But Sandy brooded about the relationship, she became depressed, and she attempted suicide by taking an overdose of tranquilizers. While she was in the hospital she told a social worker about the incest, and that led to Ed's arrest and conviction. Now Sandy blames herself because her father's in prison, she still has bouts of severe depression, and she's still under psychiatric care.

Ed is a mild mannered, slightly built man who looks his age. He's a master carpenter, he was being paid top wages at the time of his arrest, and he and his family were living comfortably in a middle-class neighborhood. He says he drank beer on weekends but he never got drunk, and he denies use of drugs.

In therapy Ed talked about his own childhood. He grew up on a farm in West Virginia, the youngest boy in a family of six. His three oldest brothers left home while he was growing up, so most of his memories are about his sisters, one two years older, the other a year younger. He cries or he trembles when he remembers his father, the frequent beatings, being made to feel worthless. He has one of those nonverbal memories of the infant, a picture of his father beating his mother with a stick until she was covered with blood. By the time he was five years old his mother was dead, and within a few months he had a step-mother. He said she was a "cold" woman who would delight in "telling" his father his every mischief and then sit back smugly while his father beat him. If his father was ever anything but cruel, he didn't remember it. He remembered once when his favorite old mare was unable to pull a loaded wagon how his father beat the horse to make her move, and when she still couldn't pull the load, how his father set a fire under her, and he remembered his screams mingling with the screams of the mare and how his father beat him for crying. He remembered that his father had sex with both of his sisters, that his sisters were too terrified to protest, and that his step-mother was smugly aware.

In late adolescence Ed ran away from home and "bummed" around the country. Finally, he settled in western Maryland, not too far from his father's home, driven, as he would be driven for all of his life, to make some sort of peace with his father . . . but that never happened. Even though his father is now dead, the ghost of the man still haunts Ed. He wants to believe that his father somehow loved him, but his every memory is of abuse and neglect. He can now express his hatred of his step-mother, but he can't hate his father without guilt.

Ed married, Sandy was born, and eventually he and his family moved to Baltimore, and it was here that he settled down and learned his trade. But he became so involved in work and making a lot of money, working many hours overtime, that he neglected his family. He could say now, in therapy, that he was acting like "lord and master," that his wife had to cater to his every whim, and that she should have been grateful for the good living he was providing. Instead, she found another man to supply her emotional needs, and before long she and Ed were separated and then divorced. She got custody of Sandy, and though Ed had visiting rights, for several years after he didn't see his daughter.

Ed married again, and two boys were born to this marriage. But this marriage was a repeat of the last even though it lasted longer. Ed was a "workaholic" and he neglected the emotional needs of his wife and children, and there seemed always to be tension and arguments in his home. But Ed declared, "I never hit my wife and I never hit my kids. I'm not my father." Still, it was an unhappy home, and it was this home Sandy started to visit when she was eight years old.

Sandy was a morose child. She didn't like her step-father, and she now had a half-brother whom her mother adored. Sandy felt pushed aside in her own home, but her real father was different. She was certain of his love. And it was true. For some reason, the feelings Ed couldn't express to his wife and children, he could express to Sandy.

Had anyone noticed then, perhaps it might have been felt that their caresses were too tender, but no one seemed to notice anything "abnormal," and it was very much later before Ed could admit the sexuality of the relationship. When pushed in therapy, he said angrily, "All right, I'd hug her and get a hard-on. That's normal. I didn't *do* anything." Only he did, but that admission came later still. "We played tickling games, and I'd tickle her between her legs . . . I'd let her do it to me. I'd find reasons to get her undressed . . . She liked that. She liked to undress for me."

It was about this time Ed caught his wife with another man, an almost classic scene of finding them naked in bed. In his rage he beat and bloodied the man, but he still couldn't strike his wife though the urge to hurt her was strong within him. He demanded that she leave him, and she left taking the two boys with her. She later filed for divorce.

Ed was alone in the house now, but Sandy still came to visit him. When she wasn't with him, he was lonely. Why, he wondered. Two wives. He gave so much to two wives, worked so hard for two families, and they couldn't be loyal to him. He gave so much, and he got betrayal in return. No one had ever loved him. Except Sandy. That was the one, constant love.

Sandy had just turned 12 when he took her into a bedroom to teach her about the difference between the sexes. They both got undressed.

"I didn't have to force her or anything. Like she knew what was going to happen, and she wanted it to happen. I didn't penetrate her the first time . . . It was beautiful . . . It wasn't dirty . . . I'll never believe it was dirty."

So the needy child and the man in need came together, and the man hurt the person he loved most in all the world. For I have no reason to disbelieve Ed—that he perceived the relationship as one of love, not lust—and then we must wonder at his ability to blind himself to what he was really doing. Even now, knowing that Sandy has been hurt, he still finds it had to believe there is anything wrong with his romantic love for his daughter, and he still loves her in the same romantic way. He's just not going to have sex with her anymore.

It's probably not accurate to call Ed a pedophile. Aside from his one daughter, his sexual interests are all adult heterosexual. His therapy suggests that the issue of "control" is a most important theme in his life: as an employee, he was careful to treat his supervisors with all respect; as a prisoner, he never breaks a rule or regulation; as a man, he never argues with authority figures; but as a husband and father, he must be dominant. When he perceives others as being powerful, he submits; he then demands submission from those he perceives to be weaker than himself. Throughout his life he has tried and failed to command love. Throughout his life there has been a desperate need for love. And then there was Sandy, her love given naturally, but it wasn't enough, and it didn't meet the need.

We see Ed's case repeated many times with only minor variations. Almost invariably, the incest offender has had at best an unhappy childhood, his marriages are failures, his adult heterosexual relationships unsatisfying, he may have a "masculine" occupation but he doesn't socialize with men, and if he has more than one daughter, he is likely to sexualize them all as they reach a preferred age. But aside from this criminal behavior, he is also likely to be a law-abiding citizen. It is extremely rare for him to go looking for children outside of the home. Once caught, he rarely recidivates.

The incest offender, therefore, doesn't fit our picture of the chronic criminal. That he is a deliberate criminal and that he willfully puts himself at risk when he breaks the incest taboo is beyond question, for in spite of his many rationalizations he knows he's doing wrong. But he's not a predator, and he usually responds to treatment and/or punishment. There's probably little need for him to go to prison except for punishment for he's probably done all the damage he's ever going to do, and the protection of society is not at issue. He has unquestionably hurt a child or children, but he is not so much a dangerous man as a pathetic man.

However, just because the crime is incest doesn't mean there aren't other pedophiliac interests. Phil is also an incest offender, his history very much like Ed's, but he had a strong sexual interest in children long before he molested his daughter, and he had secreted in his home a large collection of child pornography. Tom is in prison for molesting his daughter, but he has also molested neighborhood children. Sometimes the line between incest-only and generalized pedophilia is very sharp, and sometimes there's a lot of shading.

The Child Molester

There are a number of mistaken ideas about pedophilia, those which Groth, Burgess, Birnbaum, and Gary (1978) call "myths," so before we get to theory, let's start by defining the population of child molesters.

Myth #1: The child molester is a dirty old man. In fact, most child molesters begin to act out while they're still in their teens, but a "pedophilia" problem may not be recognized then because the disparity in age is still not too great. The median age of pedophiles who enter the criminal justice system for the first time is about thirty, clustering between twenty-five and thirty-five, with a range from the late teens to over fifty.

Myth #2: The offender is a stranger to his victim. In fact, in a study by Spencer and Dunkle (1986), 85% of the perpetrators were known to the child. Showers et al. (1983) report that 79% of their boy victims knew the abuser. Groth et al. (1978) report that in their sample only 29% of the offenders selected victims who were strangers, and in 14% of the cases the offender was a member of the child's immediate family. Finkelhor (1987) reports that fathers and stepfathers are involved in about 7% to 8% of the cases, other family members in roughly 40% of the cases, and other people known to the child in roughly 50% of the cases, which leaves only 2% or 3% molested by strangers.

Myth #3: The child molester is retarded. In fact, there is absolutely no evidence to suggest that this is so. The IQ of child molesters tends to follow the normal curve.

Myth #4: The child molester is an alcoholic or drug-addicted. Actually, many offenders claim intoxication as an excuse for their behavior, but true substance dependency is rare. Alcohol abuse is more frequent than drug abuse, and there is evidence (Finkelhor, 1987) that it is most prevalent in cases of incest.

Myth #5: The child molester is a sexually frustrated person, and he turns to children because he has no other sexual outlet. In fact, roughly 50% of all molesters are married or otherwise heterosexually active. When children are the exclusive sex object, it is because children are the preferred sex object.

Myth #6: The child molester progresses over time to increasingly violent acts. In fact, the molester probably isn't going to become any more violent than he already is. The evidence (Abel, Mittleman, & Becker, 1983; Longo & Groth, 1983) suggests that as juveniles the potential molester is likely to be involved in such paraphilic activities as exhibitionism and voyeurism, and that he progresses from this to pedophilia. Some pedophiles (roughly 10%) are sadistic and find pleasure in hurting the child, but most pedophiles entice or seduce children into committing sexual acts and they are truly distressed by the thought of hurting a child. (Of course, they're also adept a denying there is any psychic trauma.)

Myth #7: Little girls are more likely to become victims than little boys. Absolutely false. In the Groth et al. (1978) study, 51% of the offenders selected only female children; 28% selected only male children; and 21% selected both boys and girls. Generally, it's felt that the incidence of boy-molestation has been underreported, but that's changing. Spencer and Dunkle (1986) report on 1,748 children who were evaluated after being molested, indicating that in a five-year period the reported incidence of boy-molestation rose from 5% to 14%. In the Showers et al. (1983) study of victims, 13% were boys.

Myth #8: Child molesters are mentally ill. In fact, Knopp (1984) suggests that less than 5% of pedophiles can be considered psychotic, and about 29% may be antisocial personalities. Most investigators agree that the vast majority of pedophiles have no outstanding psychiatric illness other than their deviant interest in children.

From all of the studies of child molesters two very salient facts do emerge:

Fact #1: The population of pedophiles is extremely heterogeneous. According to Knopp (1984):

> Realistically, the sex offender may be a close relative, friend, or acquaintance rather than stranger; an older person or a youth as young as eight years of age; wealthy or poor; a Caucasian or a person of color; gay or straight; literate or illiterate; able or disabled; religious or nonreligious; a professional, white- or blue-collar, or unemployed worker; a person with an extensive criminal record or one with no recorded offense history. (p. 4)

In short, the child molester could be anyone.

Fact #2: The number of offenses committed by paraphiliacs is considerably higher than cases reported to officials or reflected in official statistics. According to Abel, Mittleman, and Becker (1983), their sample of 411 paraphiliacs attempted 238,711 sex crimes and completed 218,900 of them. There were 232 child molesters in the sample whose victims were less than fourteen years old; they made 55,250 attempts, had 38,727 completions, and there were 17,585 victims. On the average, each offender had attempted 238.2 child molestations and had completed 166.9 molestations on 75.8 victims.

The numbers are staggering, but this study merely documents what clinicians always "knew." One of my pedophile patients liked to play with boys aged nine to eleven, he'd engage them in some body contact activity, and he'd reach orgasm by rubbing against them. Since neither he nor the boy was exposed, the child often didn't know he was being molested. This man admitted that in the two years before his arrest he set himself a goal of a child a day . . . and he met it. It's not only the numbers that are staggering, the obsession with children can be beyond belief, and perhaps the compulsive nature of the aberrant drive can lead us to a dynamic formulation.

A BRIEF LOOK AT THEORY

Several suggestions have been proposed as to how we might type pedophiles, and the idea that seems to have caught on most is that of the "fixated" and the "regressed" pedophile (Groth & Birnbaum, 1978; Groth, Hobson, & Gary, 1982). They are distinguished as follows:

The fixated type first evidences a sexual interest in children during adolescence, and he never matures beyond that interest. Generally, he's attracted to boys so he's often labeled a "homosexual pedophile," but that label is misleading. The sex object is "child," not "male," and these men have little inclination toward adult homosexual relations. Their pedophilic behavior often has a compulsive, driven quality, they are virtually obsessed by thoughts of boys, and their offenses are planned and premeditated. Very often there is no indication of any other psychopathology in their lives, but they are usually unmarried and they may have poor social skills. Among pedophiles, they tend to have the highest recidivism rates.

The regressed type, on the other hand, doesn't begin to demonstrate a sexual interest in children until after he reaches adulthood, and frequently some distress occurs which precipitates the behavior. Most of the victims are female, the offense is often alcohol-related, and the first offense may be impulsive and unpremediated. After the first offense, the offending becomes easier, and though these men will maintain normal heterosexual relationships, they may still occassionally seek out child partners. On the whole, they are less driven than the fixated type, and their treatment prognosis is better.

The fixated-regresed typology is probably most useful in that it leads to an understanding of pedophilia as a developmental phenomenon: that is, (1) a fixation or blockage at some early developmental stage which inhibits emotional growth, or (2) a return to some earlier stage in development as a method of problem solving. Thus, the fixated pedophile is said to identify with the child-victim and to become himself a child in the encounter; while the regressed pedophile uses the child as a substitute for the adult relationship, in effect making the child a pseudoadult.

This typology isn't the only way to explain pedophilia. Araji and Finkelhor (1985) reviewed the empirical research and concluded that there were four broad theories, each of which concentrated on a particular dynamic: (1) emotional congruence, or why the adult had an emotional need to relate to a child; (2) sexual arousal, or why the adult could become sexually aroused by a child; (3) blockage, or why alternative sources of sexual and emotional gratification are not available; and (4) disinhibition, or why the adult is not deterred from such an interest by normal prohibitions. Each question raised is valid and is probably part of a total psychodynamic package, and we can speculate that the relative importance of each dynamic varies from individual to individual.

Let me illustrate the above with a few case histories. The first is a fixated pedophile.

Jeff has his doctorate in education, but he has limited classroom teaching experience. He became an administrator early in his career, and by the time of his first arrest at the age of 45 he was an Assistant Superintendent of Schools. His arrest came in the course of a police "crackdown" on a ring of juvenile male prostitutes; he was "fingered" as one of their steady customers. With the aid of a good lawyer he was able to avoid publicity, and he even managed to keep his job because it was a position that didn't bring him into contact with children. But his wife of 20 years left him and started divorce proceedings.

Jeff moved into a one bedroom luxury apartment. He was on probation, and he was required to be in psychotherapy. He told his therapist that he now had his life back under control. He described his involvement with boys as an "accident" or an "adventure," something that was different sexually but didn't really mean anything, and since he only went with prostitutes, he figured he hadn't hurt anyone. He said he and his wife were probably going to separate anyhow; in fact, since they hadn't been sexually intimate for years, she was probably the cause of his looking for prostitutes. He was angry with her because she wouldn't let him visit with his children, a 16 year old girl and a 10 year old boy, implying that he might molest them; but he didn't think of his children sexually, he just wasn't that kind of man.

In spite of his arrest and conviction his career went well, and most people believed that he had had a "little problem" that was now being treated and would go away. But a year later he was spotted in the company of a known boy-prostitute, his probation officer investigated, and new charges were filed. This time his apartment was searched, and the police found hundreds of photographs of nude boys between the age of 8 and 11, some of them specifically erotic. Jeff then confessed to numerous liasons with boys stretching back over a period of three years, and during the year he was on probation and in treatment, the activity had actually increased. This time there were headlines, Jeff was fired from his job, and he was eventually sentenced to 5 years in prison.

Now he became more honest in therapy. He recalled his first sexual experience, when he was 11 years old, and he was enticed into committing fellatio on a 15-year-old. He said he did it a few more times with other boys, but when he got to be 13 he decided he didn't want to be "queer" and the behavior stopped. He dated girls, there was heavy petting which he said he enjoyed, but he was over 20 before his first sexual intercourse. It was when he was in high school that he first started to notice 9 and 10 year old boys and how "cute" they were, and he began to fantasize seeing them naked. But that was "queer," and he wasn't going to be "queer."

For the next 20 years Jeff fought against his aberrant sexual interests. Early on he recognized that he went into teaching so he could be around children, and he said, "Being in a classroom with them all day long was driving me crazy. I wanted to touch them. I could hardly keep my hands off of them. I had to get away from them." He was going to graduate school at the time, and before long he was able to transfer to educational administration. Then, removed from daily temptation, he forced himself to become heterosexually active. "I don't dislike women," he said, but during his years of marriage he was plagued by many periods of impotence. "I'd have to fantasize about boys in order to have relations with my wife." At one point in his life he thought he might really be gay and that all his troubles would be over if he'd just admit his homosexuality, so he went to gay bars and made a few contacts. "I hated it," he said. "A hairy body is a turn-off. I couldn't get an erection." Finally he had to admit that only little boys were a "turn-on," he knew that seducing them was wrong and harmful, and he was forced to live with the misery of his desires. He became deeply depressed and he went to a psychiatrist, but after two years of analysis he was as tormented as ever by his "unholy" desires, so he quit therapy. He wasn't so depressed now but the obsessive thoughts remained. Eventually he convinced himself that if he only went after boys who were already prostitutes he wouldn't be hurting them. "And once I started to do it," he said, "I couldn't stop. With the boys, I was fulfilled for the first time in my life. Nothing else mattered."

As Jeff became more involved in therapy he talked about his parents and his early childhood experiences. He spoke of ambitious parents, both of whom were involved in careers, neither of whom had time for their children. The feeling he remembered most from his childhood was loneliness. He remembered that when the 15-year-old had seduced him, he felt a little scared and guilty at first, but he also had a sense of being desired, and he had never had that feeling before. Later, when he picked up child prostitutes, he would spend many hours with the boys doing the things they liked to do—games, arcades, building models, anything they liked to to—and that was almost more important than the sex, but the sex was that "extra" way to show them how much he loved them. He eventually came to recognize that though he had always handled adult responsibilities in an adult way, he was never really comfortable with adults of either sex, that he was most happy when he was a boy again with his boys. There was a return to that period in his life when he had missed happiness—in a futile attempt to find it.

Reports in the literature (e.g., Groth, 1979; Seghorn, Prentky, & Boucher, 1987; Tingle, Bernard, Robbins, Newman, & Hutchinson, 1986) indicate that many child molesters were themselves sexually molested as children, and though these are primarily samples of prisoners, one must pay attention to the numbers (usually between 40% and 60%). Being molested probably doesn't "cause" a man to become a molester, but his own sexualized childhood may contribute to his ability to sexualize children, depending on how he perceived the experience. That is, Jeff wasn't traumatized when he was seduced at age eleven; rather, the experience was enjoyable and filled a need in his life. But the traumatic experience can lead to a different outcome.

David, a 20 year old white youth, is serving a 15 year sentence for sexually assaulting a 14 year old boy. Using a knife as a weapon, David forced the boy to perform fellatio on him.

David grew up with his mother and stepfather, and through his

early childhood he heard stories of how cruel and abusive his real
father was. David didn't believe the stories, and as he grew older he
more and more wanted to meet and get to know his own father, and
finally his mother capitulated and arranged for David to spend a
week's vacation with his father. David was 12.

The first few days were a happy father-son reunion. Then the father started drinking heavily, and one night he got David to drinking with him. When the boy was nearly drunk, he started making
love to him. David protested, and his father slapped him into submission. He removed the boy's clothes and anally raped him.

David never told anyone about this until he told me in
psychotherapy.

David made some kind of separation in his mind: he hated the man
who had sadistically assaulted him, but he couldn't hate his father. His
behavior after the assault reflects the severe trauma in that he became a
rebellious, delinquent adolescent, and sexually he had relations with
both boys and girls, not really enjoying either, never sure of who or what
he was. He was puzzled as to why he himself had raped a boy.

Turning to the regressed pedophile, the following cases aren't atypical.

Cletus is a 65 year old black man who is on probation for molesting a 12 year old girl. He said he was driving along a suburban road
when he noticed this girl walking, and he stopped and offered her a
lift. A little later he stopped the car and began to fondle her, and he
had her partially undressed before she broke away from him and
ran from the car. He says that he didn't use force, that the girl was
willing to be fondled and to play with his penis, but she became
scared when he attempted intercourse. The girl, who remembered
the tag number of his car, reported he had tried to rape her.

Cletus grew up in poverty, and everything he finally achieved in
life he achieved through hard work. He had no prior criminal record, and he abused neither drugs nor alcohol. His only failure in
life was his marriage, which he blamed on his alcoholic wife. He
said he "put up with her" until his two children were old enough to
be out on their own, and then he divorced her. "I had to pay ali-
mony, but it was worth it to be rid of her." He still sends her checks,
but he hasn't seen her for more than ten years.

He was about 55 years old when he became a "bachelor" again.
He sold his home and moved into a rooming house, and for the next
ten years he really did nothing more than work during the day and
watch television at night and on weekends. He had no social life

with either men or women. He didn't even visit his children, both now married, though he was welcome in their homes. Finally, at the age of 65, and after working 40 years for the same company, he retired, and his retirement income was more than adequate to meet all his needs. It was at this point in his life that he assaulted a 12-year-old.

Cletus was a difficult person to work with in therapy. He really was a social isolate, and he had a hard time relating to even a supportive group. He continued to insist that he was the victim, that the girl had seduced him, and he denied any sexual interest in children. He denied unusual sexual experiences in his own life. It was eventually learned that he had been heterosexually active until he was about 35 years old, and after that masturbation was his only outlet. He denied that he was lonely or bothered by anything. He denied the need for treatment. He did admit that he was wrong for allowing himself to be seduced by a child.

In the summer months Cletus would spend most of his days sitting in the park, one of many older people, but sitting apart from the others. One day a policeman told him to get out of the park. "He said I was staring at little girls," Cletus reported. "I wasn't staring at them. I was just watching them play. What's wrong with that?"

It was significant that he told this story voluntarily, for there had been no arrest and so no official record. It seemed that in spite of his many denials and his general isolation from the group, he did feel himself to be a group member, and I suspect he was looking to the group for support and control. Put under pressure by the group, he did finally admit to looking at the girls and having sexual thoughts. "But I'll never touch another one," he said. "I've learned my lesson."

Cletus remained in therapy until his probation expired, and he didn't re-offend. But in spite of the group's advice and encouragement, he continued to lead a restricted and isolated life, and at no time did he ever explore the dynamics of his behavior. How long he had pedophilic thoughts before he acted on them no one can say, although it does seem clear that his retirement brought new stresses, particularly an even greater withdrawal from social communication, and this was probably the stress that precipitated the behavior. How much of a risk he is now is also difficult to say, for he undoubtedly has pedophilic thoughts, but this is balanced by a lifetime of responsible, law-abiding behavior.

Wilbur grew up on a farm on the Eastern Shore, the 6th of 12 children, and at about the age of 8 he was initiated into sex by one of his older sisters. "Playing" with both his older and younger sisters continued until he reached puberty, and then he went out of the family for sex. His first successful intercourse was at age 13. At the age of 18 he left home and moved to the city, he received on-the-job training in a machine shop, and he eventually became a master machinist. At the age of 21 he married a 16-year-old, they settled into a typical blue-collar neighborhood, they eventually had three children, and for a while there were no unusual problems in the family. But then his wife developed a slow-growing cerebral tumor which eventually took her through dementia to death. Wilbur cared for her at home for as long as he could, but finally she had to be hospitalized. He sent his children to live with their grandparents. Feeling very lonely and unhappy now, he noticed that the 12 year old girl who lived next door also seemed to be lonely, and before long they became good, close friends, and that almost naturally led to a sexual relationship. The girl's parents found out about it and told the police.

Wilbur was convicted of a sexual offense, given a 10 year suspended sentence, and placed on probation. He was specifically ordered to stay away from the victim, so he gave up his house and moved to a room in a new neighborhood, and before long he became friendly with a 13-year-old. Wilbur said he never had sex with this girl; he said she was easy to talk to. He would eventually admit his sexual attraction to her, and he guessed that the relationship would have become sexual if her parents hadn't intervened. But they did. They complained to Wilbur's probation officer, and though he wasn't convicted of a new offense, his probation was terminated and the original 10 year sentence imposed.

I met him for the first time when he came out on parole. He was now in his early forties, a lanky white man who still had the "country" accent of his boyhood, and who admitted frankly that he still liked young girls. "But I won't touch anything under eighteen," he said. "I learned my lesson."

In fact, his first few months out of prison, he "dated" only women his own age, and in group therapy he spoke openly of his experiences. His wife had passed away while he was in prison, and now he was ready to marry again. His choice of wife: a 35 year old widow who had two prepubertal daughters. "Don't you see what you're doing?" his therapy group asked him. "Don't you see how you're setting yourself up?"

Wilbur didn't want to look at it. "I'm not a child molester," he said. "I've never been with any girl who didn't want to be with me."

With few exceptions, as we look at pedophile case history after case history, we find very little evidence of criminal behavior other than the child molesting, and we find very little evidence of physical aggression against the child. Groth and Burgess (1977) suggest that most pedophiles attempt to entice or entrap the child, that "at some level [the pedophile] cares for the child and is emotionally identified and involved with him or her" (p. 257). They also point out that there are pedophiles who force children, but in this case "sexuality appears to be in the service of a need for power" (p. 259). The violent and sadistic pedophile is fortunately rare and atypical, he may possibly be too dangerous to treat and set free, so we'll confine our discussion here to the more typical pedophile, the man who really does love children and who wouldn't dream of hurting them. Therefore, naturally, he must deny the criminality of his behavior. In his view, it is not the sexual love of children that is wrong, but rather the laws which prohibit it.

As I mentioned at the beginning, pedophiles were once called "sexual psychopaths," but taking a close look at them, there is little "psychopathic" about them other than their need to repeat the same crime over and over again and their remarkable ability to justify it. In forensic psychiatry the term "sexual psychopath" came under fire back in the 1950s, and one of the leading experts of the day was Benjamin Karpman (1954). It's interesting to look at his review of the research on the paraphilias up to 1954, because virtually nothing new has been reported in the thirty year since. I'll quote some of his findings, and I suspect it will all look familiar.

1. "There are no accurate statistics as to the number of offenses. It seems to be agreed that many that occur never come to the attention of the police" (p. 29).

2. "It is emphasized . . . that in general sex offenders do not progress from minor to serious crimes" (p. 30).

3. " . . . psychosis and mental deficiency are comparatively rare . . . " (p. 48).

4. "It is believed that sexual deviation represents a fixation at a lower stage of psychosexual development" (p. 48).

5. "The attitude that the child is an unwilling victim, is not always true; in some cases the child is the aggressor" (p. 73).

6. "The use of violence is not a determining aspect; the sexual criminal may resort to violence, but often the primary intention is to commit the act without reflecting that it may be interpreted as assault or violence" (p. 599).

After reviewing the research—and based on his own extensive experience—Karpman came to two conclusions. First, there was a distinct difference between the psychopath and the sexual offender. He said that paraphiliacs, except for their sexual behavior, may be entirely normal in every other way, and conflict with the law alone didn't make them psychopaths; he called their criminality a "neurotic symptom." He went on to say that some psychopaths did commit sexual crimes as a part of their total deviancy, but psychopaths could be distinguished from paraphiliacs by their committment to a predatory life style.

Second, and since this is Karpman's main point, let me quote him exactly:

It is the essential thesis of this presentation that in the various paraphilias we are dealing essentially with neuroses, mainly because, like neuroses, they are surface symptomatic expressions of underlying unconscious motivations. On analysis they reveal themselves as having essentially the same psychic structure as neuroses; and like neuroses, are approachable and curable by psychotherapy. (p. 398)

If we accept a dynamic formulation of this sort, then the phenomonology of the pedophile-child encounter takes on a new significance. However we perceive the incident, is it dynamically an act of aggression? However we think the child should respond, how in fact does the child respond? Of interest in this regard is what Finkelhor (1987) reports as the five high risk factors for child sexual abuse: (1) a child who is living without one of his biological parents; (2) a child whose mother is unavailable either as a result of employment outside of the home, disability, or illness; (3) a child who is living with parents who are in conflict; (4) a child who is being subjected to extremely punative discipline; and (5) a child who is living with a stepfather. In short, the child most at risk is the child who feels most deprived of adult love, comfort, and security. Could it be that the pedophile—however inappropriately— often fills this void?

As the research on the effects of sexual abuse indicates, childrens' reactions to the experience don't follow any predictable pattern. It's a bad experience for the child not because he *will* suffer but because he's placed at high risk *to* suffer. The pedophile's perception that the child enjoys the experience and that after initiation may even become seductive could be accurate, a behavioral response of the victim that would reinforce the pedophile's denial of any long-term negative effects. The needy child may also feel and express love for the pedophile, accepting sex as the price to pay for caring, and while this certainly puts the child at risk, the immediate perception is that of a loving relationship. If we look only at the phenomenology of the encounter, we may have no reason to disbelieve the pedophile's perceptions, which is not the same as saying that we accept them as justifications. To think this way in the course of psychotherapy means that we give less emphasis to the power-aggression dynamic and less emphasis to the predatory nature of the crime; we believe the pedophile's assertion that he wants to love and not hurt children; and we begin to get some sense of the emotional vacuum in the pedophile's life.

At this point I think there is a need to make a clear distinction between the "occasional" and the "repetitive" child molester, which in a sense may also be thought of as the "noncriminal" and "criminal" pedophile. What is probably most true of the "occasional" molester is that while the sexual attraction to children may be ever present, acting out probably won't occur until some stress and/or emotional upset precipitates it. Respect for the illegality, if not immorality, of the act is recognized; the gamble to satisfy the desire is not lightly taken, and feelings of guilt alone may be enough to end the behavior. We are dealing with men for whom any aspect of criminality is ego-dystonic.

However, when we deal with the "repetitive" child molester, I tend to see this as a variation of "the will to fail" in that it is not a persistent dynamic in the pedophile's life but is, rather, transient. That is, the pedophile does succeed, he does cope, and he handles most aspects of his life reasonably, even though the success isn't enjoyed because of the persistent, underlying desire to escape from the world of adults. Then, at some point in his life—sooner for some than for others—he becomes willing to gamble all, willing to accept failure as the price, in order to satisfy his paraphilic cravings, and at this time he is as much psychopathic as any chronic criminal. But it is a transient state, it's duration variable depending on other factors in the personality. If the state does seem to be more or less permanent—the case of Harry in Chapter 2, for example—then we might guess that the character structure really is psychopathic, but generally, after massive failure, the pedophile is ready to regain some control of his life. Sometimes he has to "hit bottom"—and the addiction analogy is apt—before he's able to make use of any treatment. Like psychopaths, his will to fail is also a plea for structure and rescue; unlike psychopaths, he doesn't need to be forever rescued.

Except for those pedophiles who are also psychopathic, I don't believe pedophiles like or use prison in the same way as chronic criminals. Prison is a punishing experience for them, but it's not curative. It helps them to gain control and to take fewer chances with their lives, but it doesn't stop the child molesting. The pedophile becomes more careful. The literature on the recidivism of pedophiles, which suggests that the rate is low, is misleading. Groth, Longo, and McFadin (1982) report that their sample of child molesters committed about five undetected molestations for every detected molestation; that is, five additional victims but probably numerous contacts with each one. Soothill and Gibbens (1978) point out that the reported recidivism rate of pedophiles is low because the follow-up periods are only three or four years, but that changes when the follow-up period is ten years. A study of sex offenders in Norway (Grunfeld & Noreik, 1986), which did include a ten-year follow-up, indicated that child abusers were caught offending for the second time on the average of forty-six months after their release from prison. Prison alone isn't the answer for pedophiles, if it is ever the answer for anyone. We turn now to a consideration of treatment strategies.

ASPECTS OF THE TREATMENT PROCESS

The treatment of pedophilia is related to both the treatment of psychopathy and the treatment of the addictions. As I've indicated, the "cured" psychopath is very rarely a "normal" man; that is, he carries with him for all his life the burden of intractable character defects which prevent his full participation in the human experience, and often the most we can hope for is that he does no more harm. Similarly, it is the rare pedophile who will be "cured" of his sexual interest in children, and often the best we can hope for is behavioral control. In a sense we come back to the question posed at the beginning of this chapter: Are deviant sexual fantasies *alone* enough to indicate a deviant personality? That's of more than academic interest, for the behavioral therapists tend to answer it one way and psychodynamic therapists another way, and the answer leads to treatment techniques and expectations.

Pedophilia is like the addictions in that there is an obsessive-compulsive quality to the search for children and the need for children, and very likely the learning theory model of the addictions helps to explain both the onset of the condition and the fairly high relapse rate. Therefore, as in the addictions, a multimodal approach to treatment is probably required for the best results. The nature of these "modes" depends once again upon our essential conceptualization of the condition. Laws (1987) names three problem areas which should be addressed in the treatment of pedophiles.

These are: (1) *deviant sexual arousal*, the tendency to become sexually aroused to inappropriate sexual objects; (2) *deviant sexual cog-*

nitions, the thought processes used by the offender to justify and support his deviant sexual behavior; and (3) *a strong tendency toward relapse* following treatment for sexual deviation. (p. 1)

The first of these, the treatment of deviant sexual arousal, is problematic for dynamic psychiatry, and it's based on an assumption that probably has little validity. Abel (cited in Knopp, 1984) says, "I do not know the cause of child molesting, but I do believe the reasons for this and most other sexual deviations rest with an arousal pattern" (p. 38). So believing, the behaviorists have developed a number of techniques for reducing (eliminating?) arousal to deviant stimuli, the most popular of which seem to be olfactory aversion and masturbation satiation. Pithers and Laws (in press) write:

In olfactory aversive conditioning paradigms, arousal to stimuli depicting sexual abuse is paired with a noxious odor. Typically, presentation of the unpleasant odor leads to rapid detumescence. After repeated pairings of the aversive odor and deviant stimulus, deviant stimuli no longer elicit arousal. (p. 7)

McGrath and Carey (1987) describe the masturbatory satiation technique as follows:

In this procedure, deviant fantasies are extinguished through satiation or boredom. In the privacy of his own home, the offender is asked to masturbate to orgasm to a nondeviant fantasy, which is spoken aloud into a tape recorder. Following orgasm, he masturbates for 45 minutes while repeating his deviant fantasies into the tape recorder. This course of treatment lasts for about 20 sessions at the rate of two to four sessions per week. The procedure has the effect of rendering the offender's deviant fantasies extremely boring and therefore not stimulating. (p. 30)

Several problems with techniques of this sort exist. They unquestionably do inhibit arousal *in the laboratory situation* and possibly even during the course of treatment, but the behavioral therapies, historically, have never been noted for their long-term effectiveness when the patients have severe characterological problems (Barley, 1986; Marks, 1981; Schwitzgebel, 1971). The most disturbing problem is the assumption upon which the treatment is based, that deviant arousal and criminal behavior are congruous, and nothing could be further from the truth. The willingness to repeatedly perform criminal acts has absolutely nothing to do with penile tumescence. Rapists, for example, very often do not achieve penetration because they can't get erect. It's not the penis that commits the crime, it's the person to whom it's attached. Groth (1985) expresses the psychodynamic view:

> We don't believe that the primary motivation for sexual offenses is sexual desire, that the sexual offender is committing his crime primarily out of sexual desire any more than we think an alcoholic is drinking primarily because he's thirsty. We see this behavior as the sexual expression of many non-sexual needs or issues in his life that have remained unresolved or unaddressed. (p. 7)

Nonetheless, behavioral technology has been introduced into many treatment programs (Knopp, Rosenberg, & Stevenson, 1986), and one technique, penile plethysmography, could possibly be of value to all clinicians. Basically, the subject fits a transducer around his penis, a device which detects changes in the circumference of the penis, and he is exposed to either audio or visual erotic stimuli. The device measures even minute changes in circumference, these are expressed as changes in electrical resistance, and these resistance changes are plotted and graphed. The assumption is that however much the subject may deny deviant interests, the penis doesn't lie. Though in fact it may. (For a comprehensive discussion of penile plethysmography, see Laws, 1987; Pithers & Laws, in press.)

Abel, Mittleman, and Becker (1983) suggest that when there is one paraphilia there are probably others. For example, in their sample of 232 child molesters, physiological assessment of their sexual arousal revealed these other paraphilic interests: rape 16.8%; exhibitionism 29.7%; voyeurism 13.8%; frotteur 8.6%; sadism 5.6%; transvestism 3.4%; masochism 3.0%; fetish 3.0%; and transsexualism 0.4%. It's suggested that these deviant interests would not have been uncovered by self-reports alone.

The use of the plethysmograph in both evaluation and treatment is described in a great many articles (e.g., Abel & Blanchard, 1976; Earls & Marshall, 1983; Laws & Osborn, 1983; Travin, Bluestone, Coleman, Cullen, & Mellela, 1986), and one doesn't dispute its value as an assessment device. However, as a measure of the efficacy of treatment there is great potential for abuse if treatment success is defined as reduced arousal to deviant sexual stimuli and/or increased arousal to sexually appropriate stimuli. It's conceivable that a corrections system someplace someday may use plethysmograph results to make parole decisions, and that would be tragic. For the plethysmograph simply indicates what the deviant interests are; it does not assess the potential for deviant behavior.

Among the therapies which place emphasis upon reducing physiological responsiveness there is treatment with the antiandrogen medroxyprogesterone acetate (MPA), also known as Depo-Provera, a drug which decreases serum testosterone levels significantly. Berlin and Krout (1986) write: "The idea of using MPA in the case of pedophiles is to try to decrease the intensity of his sexual cravings, thereby, hopefully, making it easier for him to successfully resist unwanted temptations. The drug cannot change the nature of his sexual orientation" (p. 25).

The articles by Berlin and various associates (Berlin, 1983, 1985; Berlin & Coyle, 1981; Berlin & Krout, 1986; Berlin & Meinecke, 1981) all suggest that there may be a physiological basis to pedophilia, though I don't find the data very convincing because of flaws in sampling and research design. However, Berlin doesn't restrict use of MPA to only those men who have abnormally high testosterone levels; rather, it is used much in the manner of a psychotropic medication in that theoretically it reduces obsessional sexual preoccupations. That has yet to be demonstrated. What has been demonstrated (Cooper, 1986) by plethysmogrpah examination is that while MPA does reduce serum testosterone levels, it does not reduce arousal to deviant stimuli. Though Berlin has been the champion of Depo-Provera for a number of years now, he has published no treatment follow-up and recidivism studies. He does report: "The data . . . shows clearly that in most cases, when paraphilic patients discontinue medication they relapse" (p. 110).

Like the addict, the pedophile will often complain that it is the law that is wrong, that his behavior is not harmful to anyone, and that he is "criminal" only in the sense that he is the victim of an irrational morality. Cognitions of this sort help him to break the law in the first place, and if they aren't changed, they help him to re-offend. So virtually every treatment program in the country, whatever its primary orientation, dynamic, behavioral, or medical, includes components aimed at cognitive restructuring. They may include sexuality education, victim empathy groups, and other more or less didactic forms of psychotherapy. Some programs also directly address the essential character structure of the pedophile with such components as social skills training and assertiveness training. Still, basic to every treatment program, is some form of group and/or individual psychotherapy. (See Groth, 1983; Knopp, 1984; McGrath & Carey, 1987.)

With few exceptions, even fixated pedophiles do have other sexual outlets, most often adult heterosexual, sometimes adult homosexual, and if these outlets aren't as satisfying as children, they are at least a sexual alternative that's probably better than just masturbation. It's sometimes possible to reinforce and make more attractive these other sexual outlets—either behaviorally or dynamically—but it's rarely possible to convince the pedophile that sex with children isn't pleasurable. It was and he remembers that it was. He may now be convinced that sex with children is damaging to the child, certainly damaging to himself, and he may know both intellectually and emotionally that he can never again commit those acts—but children will still be perceived as sex objects. Whatever appropriate sexual outlets he now may have, children will still tempt him. To this extent he's like an addict, and the circumstances associated with his offending may act as conditioned stimuli and lead him to re-offend. If, for example, he habitually found his victims at parks and arcades, he will have to avoid parks and arcades. Or if his offending was associated with stresses in his life and changes in mood, he will have to learn how to monitor his emotional state so as to take preventive action before it's too late. He must be continually aware of those high risk situations which can lead to relapse. This is all part of the relapse prevention model (Pithers, Marques, Gibat, & marlatt, 1983).

The treatment of pedophilia has this in common with the treatment of all criminals: whatever the technique, institutional treatment alone is not enough; treatment must follow the man into the community. This may (should?) include strict parole supervision, but, as always, it's not the externally controlling authority that will make the inevitable difference, but rather the trusting relationship that leads to internal controls.

CONCLUSION

When Karpman (1954) reviewed the literature on the treatment of the paraphilias, he wasn't at all pessimistic—unless, of course, the paraphiliac was also psychopathic. This was all before the behavior therapies and MPA, and the psychodynamic therapies were thought to be quite effective. However, there is a bias in favor of the essentially noncriminal paraphiliac, and I think that distinction, criminal versus noncriminal, is still important. That is, we are not dealing with the same dynamic processes when we deal with the pedophile who has acted out once or twice versus the pedophile who acts out repeatedly. Even if their fantasy life is the same, it is the willingness to transgress, the willingness to put the self at risk, that makes the difference. Neither medication nor the behavior therapies address this issue. In a sense, "noncriminal" pedophilia is much like reactive addiction in that virtually any treatment will stop the offending, but a treatment which does not address the criminality of the chronic offender is worthless. Also like the addict, we can't infer criminality in the first-time offender even though his pedophilic activities are associated with many psychopathic traits: activities to obtain children for sex must be as devious as activities to obtain illegal drugs.

In that the first-time child molester is an unknown—and given that he has no record of other criminal behavior—does it make any sense to put him in prison? Karpman (1954) says: "Those who maintain prison will redeem the sexual criminal are greatly in the minority. The failure of prison as a deterrent to crime is stressed" (p. 268). Macindoe (cited in Knopp, 1984) states: "I take it as an incontrovertible fact that prison is degrading, antitherapeutic, psychologically and psychosocially destructive and damaging, and to be avoided at all costs if treatment is to be effective" (p. 119). Berlin and Krout say that "there is nothing about being in prison that can change the nature of the pedophile's sexual orientation" (p. 22). On the other hand, the community's right to be safe is a primary issue: for every pedophile who is an outpatient treatment failure, there is another child victim. It becomes a gamble any way you look at it. Probation and outpatient treatment puts the community immediately at risk, but since imprisonment isn't likely to cure anything, it simply delays the risk for a year or two. It seems to me that probation and treatment is the better gamble.

However, it's an entirely different matter when we consider outpatient treatment failures and multiple offenders. By this time we are dealing with people who have not learned from their punishing experiences in the criminal justice system, possibly people who are obsessed with their deviant sexuality. We may consider them either in terms of the psychopathic paradigm or the psychoneurotic paradigm. In the first instance, psychopathy, we may infer a personality structure characterized by hedonism, narcissism, disregard for the rights of others, affective and empathic incapacity, and that need for safety in structure which the prison is so able to provide; we are dealing with criminality, and child molesting is as much symptom for these men as bank robbery is for other criminals. In the second instance, psychoneurosis, the sexual deviance has the same quality as any other obsessional symptom in that the symptom is designed to mask the problem; that is, so long as the individual is preoccupied with sexual thoughts, sexual behavior, and the social consequences of his behavior, he does not have to consider other aspects of his life functioning, and he has a ready excuse for all of his personal, interpersonal, and social failures. To characterize pedophiles in either of these two ways is not to deny that they have psychosexual problems; symptom selection emerges from the organization of the total personality. Dynamic psychotherapy uncovers that organization and suggests strategies leading to reorganization. We believe that the more the individual knows about himself and the better able he is to cope with all aspects of his life, the more he will be able to exercise control over his own behavior and the less important his pedophilic symptoms will be. Of course, the psychoneurotic pedophile is infinitely more treatable than the psychopathic. Though the sexual attraction to children may remain in either case, the psychopathic will to fail dominates every treatment consideration.

8
Punishment and Treatment

As pure concepts, "punishment" and "treatment" are probably *not* mutually exclusive; that is, punishment can be a form of treatment that brings about behavioral change. However, we don't live in a world of pure concepts, and the laboratory experience doesn't always generalize nicely to practical application. Furthermore, the behavioral sciences, which utilize punishment as one tool in a battery of teaching tools, are more likely to be concerned with the modification of man's behavior than the reformation of his moral character; punishment is applied to extinguish "undesirable," not "bad," behavior, and to imply "goodness" or "badness" to any behavior may be more a matter of social control than of morality. But the concept of punishment as a criminal sanction invariably includes some degree of moralizing, for within the criminal justice system punishment is accepted not only as a tool to change behavior, but also as a means of exacting retribution; that is, to inflict pain is an end in itself, for the criminal merits his suffering. (For a discussion of the philosophical and legal implications of punishment, see Gerber & McAnany, 1977; Grupp, 1971.)

Foucault (1977) traces the development of the modern prison, indicating that in spite of the reassuring words of the humanists, prisons are meant to be a painful experience. He writes:

From the point of view of the law, detention may be a mere deprivation of liberty. But the imprisonment that performs this function

137

has always involved a technical project. The transition from the public execution, with its spectacular rituals, its art mingled with the ceremony of pain, to the penalties of prisons buried in architectural masses and guarded by the secrecy of administrations, is not a transition to an undifferentiated, abstract, confused penality; it is the transition from one art of punishing to another, no less skillful one. It is a technical mutation. (p. 257)

It's generally felt that the punishment of criminals serves four desirable purposes: retribution, deterrence, prevention, and reformation. There can be nothing but an emotional or philosophical argument for retribution, but the law often looks to psychology to otherwise justify punishment. However, there is a difference between punishment as a tool of the behavioral sciences and punishment as a weapon of justice. In either case, punishment is always defined as something "unpleasant," either the application of pain or the denial of pleasure, but the behavioral scientist will be sure to include in his definition something like this, " . . . as pain and pleasure are perceived by the subject." Over the years experimental psychology has demonstrated that punishment is not a simple stimulus-response concept, that it has many ramifications, and, in human learning, to be effective it must take into consideration the biosocial and psychological nature of the individual. (For a review of the literature, see Johnston, 1972.) It would be unfair to say that justice punishes indiscriminately, in that judges are given some leeway to impose nonpenal versus penal sentences, but the range of alternatives is small, and the leeway narrows with the severity of the crime and with repeated offenses, until inevitably the public will to exact vengeance impinges upon any juristic moderation. Thus (putting aside any discussion of the death penalty), imprisonment is presumed to be the ultimate sanction, and the longer the sentence the more severe the punishment. More often than not the sentence—the punishment—is related to the crime and not to the criminal; it is punishment in its retributive sense and not in its corrective sense because it ignores individual differences. Zilboorg (1954) points out that there is a difference between the active suffering that leads to reform as opposed to the passive acceptance of suffering as one concomitant of a criminal life style that isn't going to change, which is one way to make the distinction between those who are "cured" by the prison experience and those who are chronic criminals. Or to put it in the language of the behavioral sciences, in the one instance the punishment is indeed perceived as being painful and henceforth to be avoided, while in the other instance the punishment is unpleasant but not intolerable.

The behavioral psychology of punishment is complex. If, for example, a child is coddled every time after he's been spanked, he may come to associate the pleasant stimulus with the aversive stimulus, even to the point of seeking punishment in order to reap the later reward. Similarly, chronic criminals may have to accept some physical unpleasantness in order to ensure psychological safety. In fact, their sense of the worthless self may include a need for punishment, which as pain inflicted from the outside relieves them of the responsibility to discipline themselves. Zilboorg (1954) speaks of "criminals who seek suffering and use crime only as a vehicle for masochistic gratification" (p. 97).

Imprisonment violates most of the conditions of effective punishment, if behavioral change and not simply retribution is indeed the goal. (See also Powell, 1973.) In the first place, punishment has been found to suppress a behavior most effectively when it is applied as soon as the behavior occurs; and as a corollary, the longer the delay between the behavior and the punishment, the less effective the punishment. Translating this to the criminal justice system, when the delay between arrest and trial can be several months, we can infer that the punishing power of the sentence may be diluted many times over before it is ever imposed. Add to this the "peculiar" time sense of the chronic criminal (Chapter 5), and we may then wonder how aversive a stimulus any sentence really is. We may also wonder if long sentences are really more painful than short sentences, for behavioral psychology tells us that adaptation to punishment occurs, that a punishment of given intensity will become decreasingly effective the longer it is applied. Then, out of the many variables involved in the effective use of punishment as a teaching tool, let's add just one more: punishment suppresses a behavior most effectively when there is opportunity to reward alternative behavior. Applying this principle to the prison situation, we find opportunities for reward and punishment within the structure of the prisoner society, that institutional behaviors may be molded and controlled, but we are already far removed from the original behavior, the crime, for which punishment was originally imposed. Perhaps the concept of "good time," that is, earning a reduction in sentence through good behavior, may be related to reward-punishment contingencies. If so, there is still far too great a time lag between stimulus and response for efficient learning to take place. How much is learned, for example, when "good time" cuts a thirty year sentence to twenty? In fact, there is less likely to be an association between original crime and its punishment and more likely to be an association between immediate behavior and survival in the prison milieu.

One can't say that prisons fail to punish; they do, and the experience of imprisonment is probably always painful to some degree. But when we consider the psychology of the offender, then we have to conclude that even when punishment is evenly applied, the intensity of the pain is not evenly perceived. Of interest are the studies of long-term imprisonment and prison overcrowding (cited in Chapter 5) which suggest that imprisonment does not necessarily involve significant suffering, and that there can even be a healthy adaptation to what most of us would call an inhumane and intolerable environment. One might say, therefore, that the prison-as-punishment not only fails to meet the goal of effecting positive behavioral change, it also very often fails to meet the goal of retribution in that the pain is superficial.

The recidivism rates (cited in Chapter 1) suggest that the prison-as-punishment also largely fails to meet the goals of reformation and crime prevention. Incarceration alone does not significantly reduce the tendency of the average criminal to commit new crimes upon his release. This is not because prisons are "schools for crime," as some have suggested, nor because prisons are debasing and dehumanizing, even though they are, but because incarceration, even with concomitant suffering, doesn't alter the basic character pathology of the chronic criminal. The prison is not an alien environment that destroys, nor is it a therapeutic environment that heals. The prison is an environment that nurtures.

It has been suggested (e.g., Wilson & Boland, 1977) that prisons do one thing well: incapacitate. If incarceration doesn't reduce the tendency to commit criminal acts, prolonged incarceration at least reduces the opportunity to commit them, and so there is a plea for longer sentences with little chance of early release. Statistically, a significant reduction in the crime rate can be predicted. Critics of incapacitation (e.g., Blackmore & Welsh, 1983; Clear & Barry, 1983), focus on the tremendous cost of building more prisons to hold more people for longer periods of time; and though statistically incapacitation may work, it does also tend to ignore individual differences and to treat all criminals as if they were all alike. At least when incapacitation becomes the rationale, there is no longer any need to justify punishment either therapeutically or morally. Incapacitation isn't meant to cure anything. It is a virtual acceptance of the proposition that criminality can't be cured, it overlooks the individual, and concentrates on the protection of society. One can't argue with that approach if society is willing to pay the price.

However, effective incapacitation necessarily means that there must be extremely long sentences for young offenders. Imprisoning a twenty-year-old for five, ten, or even fifteen years will not reduce his risk of re-offending upon release. The phenomenon called "burnout," seen in many chronic criminals, typically doesn't occur until about age forty. Davis (1985) suggests that offenders are people with "great energy" who use that energy to fight or otherwise subvert "the system," all energy directed outward, none in reserve for the task of personal transformation. Burnout, Davis says, "is synonymous with age-related shifts in perspective. . . . In Jungian terms, this individuation process may be seen as the 'death of the ego' whereby the unconscious notion of personal omnipotence falters" (p. 611). With respect to age and recidivism, Greenfeld (1985) reports the following:

> The younger the releasee, the higher is the rate of prison return within the first year. While an estimated 21.8% of those 18 to 24 years old at release return to prison within the first year, 12.1% of those age 25 to 34 at release, 7.1% of those aged 35 to 44, and 2.1% of those aged 45 and over do so within the first year. Similarly, though 7 years after release nearly half (49.9%) of those aged 18 to 24 at release will have returned to prison, compared to 12.4% of those 45 and over at release. Interestingly, offenders released from prison at age 45 and older demonstrate a relatively stable pattern over time, with between 1% and 2% returning to prison each year. These data indicate that the most rapid failures after release occur among the youngest releasees. (pp. 3–4)

Incapacitation as policy, therefore, requires a rethinking of current practices. Rather than giving short sentences to young first offenders and long sentences to older repeat offenders, just the reverse would have to be true. Thus, society would be faced with the problem of tax support for many young men for many long years, and would also chance that a significant number of young lives that could have been salvaged will be wasted. The argument against incapacitation, as I see it, is both fiscal and moral. The argument for it as punishment and retribution, as suggested above, is probably specious. But if applied to the right people at the right time, it will probably reduce crime.

The final argument for punishing criminals is deterrence, in the sense that the punishment of criminals will deter others from committing crimes. No conclusive evidence suggests that this is either true or not true. Simply as speculation, fear of punishment may well reinforce the ordinary person's inclination to behave in a law-abiding way, but this is a person who has already accepted familial and cultural values, who has a sense of self and self-worth, and who would not ordinarily be tempted to gamble with his life by committing felonies. None of that applies to people who are already leading criminal lives; therefore, fear of punishment has already proven to be an ineffective deterrent. However, if the concept is used in the sense of punishing the known criminal in order to deter *him* from committing another crime, then it has some utility. Prisons do "cure" some people, not by reforming them or teaching them how to lead better lives, but simply by making their lives so unpleasant they will never risk imprisonment again.

My position here is that punishment alone effects positive change in only a portion of the criminal population, and it has virtually no effect on that portion of the population that is most dangerous to society. I am not opposed to punishment as a treatment tool, and some punishing experiences are probably required in all our lives to help us reach maturity. I'm not opposed to prisons because I know many criminals present a clear and continuing danger to society. I firmly believe in restraining— incapacitating—criminals until they are no longer dangerous, but prisons on the whole don't do that. They hold dangerous men for a time, and then they release dangerous men. Surely, there must be a way to treat them so as to reduce their dangerousness.

The literature on the treatment of criminals makes for gloomy reading, and the pessimism was probably summed up by Martinson (1977) who concluded that nothing works. He reviewed 231 studies of treatment attempts in correctional settings and summarized his findings as follows: "With few and isolated exceptions, the rehabilitative efforts that have been reported so far have had no appreciable effect on recidivism" (p. 5). The "treatments" investigated were these:

1. Education and Vocational Training: Though occupational skills were often learned, and though the level of literacy often rose, neither had much to do with an individual's propensity to commit crimes.

2. Individual and/or Group Counseling: The findings suggest that some individuals benefit from this kind of treatment, but there isn't any universality of benefits.

3. Transforming The Institutional Environment: Milieu therapy programs may be more cost-effective and humane, but they don't lead to better recidivism rates.

4. Medical Treatment: Primarily this meant treatment with psychotropic medications, which had no effect on subsequent criminal behavior.

5. Sentencing: The length of sentence is not related at all to the propensity to recidivate.

6. Probation, Parole, and Community Treatment: Generally, these programs do no worse than imprisonment, and they're more cost-effective. Martinson says, "If we can't do more for (and to) offenders, at least we can safely do less" (p. 26).

However, Martinson's conclusion—nothing works—isn't actually true, for Martinson himself points out that some things work for some people some time. It's true that there is no universally effective treatment. There is no magic pill. Psychotherapy particularly shouldn't be viewed as a panacea: some prisoners need it and others don't, and some prisoners can use it and others can't.

F. J. Carney (1971) published a particularly interesting study of the effects of psychotherapy at the Walpole State Prison in Massachusetts, interesting in that the findings have since proven to have general applicability. Carney studied a group of 115 men who had had at least twenty-five weeks of psychotherapy and who had been released from the prison at least four years before; they were matched with a control group of 138 inmates who had never been in psychotherapy. It was statistically determined that the expected recidivism rate for the groups would be 68%; and it turned out that the actual recidivism rate was 53% for the treated group and 69% for the untreated group. Carney also studied another group, a group of men who had volunteered for psychotherapy but who were never actually treated before their release, and their recidivism rate was also 53%. It seems, therefore, that the *decision* to volunteer for therapy is related to some motivation to "go straight" upon release. Among Carney's other findings: (1) men with shorter criminal records tended to benefit most from therapy; (2) older inmates with long criminal histories also benefited; (3) the longer 1 and 2 above were in therapy, the better the results; (4) young inmates with long records did not benefit, and the longer they were in therapy the higher their recidivism rate; and (5) treated recidivists were generally arrested for less serious crimes.

More recent reviews of the literature (Barley, 1986; Mathias & Sindberg, 1985; Silfen, 1986), which include evaluations of both the behavioral and dynamic therapy of prisoners, continue to suggest the essential untreatability of the young multiple offender and continue to emphasize the motivational factor. It's generally felt that *differential* treatment is the key to success, that it is futile to attempt to force the patient into a theoretical model, and that perhaps success should be measured by something other than recidivism rates. With regard to the last point, treated offenders, when they are re-arrested, are usually arrested for crimes less serious, less violent than the one that originally brought them to prison, and that may be some indication of improved mental health. The problem, as has been pointed out so often, is that treatment usually doesn't follow the offender out into the community so there's little opportunity to reinforce the gains made while in prison.

Jew, Clanon, and Mattocks (1972) studied a group of 257 men who had received psychotherapy for at least a year while they were in prison, matched with a control group who had never been in therapy, and they found the following: During the first year of parole the treated group had a significantly better adjustment rate than the untreated group, but beginning in the second year the gap between the two groups began to close, and by the fourth year of follow-up the recidivism rates for the two groups were nearly identical. They concluded that there is some initial transfer of effects from therapy in prison to the parole situation but that, at best, psychotherapy in prison does little more than delay a man's return to prison.

By contrast, a report from Patuxent Institution (1973) under the Defective Delinquency Law (see Chapter 1) indicated that of 794 men recommended for commitment and treatment, 156 were not committed and so returned to a conventional prison. A follow-up (anywhere from seven to seventeen years later) disclosed that this untreated group had a recidivism rate of 81%. Of the 638 men who were committed, 186 received only in-house treatment; that is, at some point the court released them from the institution against the advice of the staff; and this group was found to have a recidivism rate of 46%. One hundred men received treatment both in the institution and while they were on parole, they were released against advice while they were on parole, and their recidivism rate was 39%. One hundred thirty-five men had both in-house treatment and treatment while on parole for at least three years and were recommended for complete release by the institution; their recidivism rate was only 7%.

Recidivism data from Patuxent under the Eligible Persons Law, which went into effect in July 1977, has not yet been published, but in-house studies are suggestive. About 44% of Patuxent's parolees are returned to the institution, mostly for technical violations of the terms and conditions of their parole, an indication of how closely their behavior is monitored. Only about 20% of the parolees are convicted of new crimes, and generally, in keeping with most studies, these are crimes of a less serious nature than the original crime.

It's often true that treatment hasn't lived up to expectations, but perhaps the expectations were too high in the first place. The chronic criminal has a wide range of severe characterological deficits, and there are limits to the changes which even intensive treatment can bring about. Perhaps we should count it as a success when our patients are "improved" to the point where they no longer commit heinous or serious crimes, and perhaps we should give them permission to fail in "little" ways. We can help them to improve the overall quality of their lives, but full participation in the human experience may be forever beyond their reach. In the end we may be left with incomplete human beings, but they're at least human beings who don't hurt anyone.

It is traditional in our culture to consider the criminal a "bad" person and to treat him as if it were his moral nature which is in need of improvement. On this assumption we justify punishment as treatment, but contrast the treatment of criminals with the treatment of the insane. At one point in time little distinction was made between criminals and the mentally ill: they were all punished. The mentally ill were seen as being just as wilful and morally deficient as criminals. It wasn't until the nineteenth century that their illness was defined as a real illness, something beyond the control of the patient, and something which required treatment rather than punishment. The treatment found to work best—in those days before the psychotropic medications—was humanistic care and concern. Not that the treatment of the mentally ill hasn't had its ups and downs—I recall visiting virtual bedlams no more than twenty years ago—but at least the *principle* was established, the mentally ill were freed from moral responsibility for their illness, and the public ceased to object to their humane care. Once people began looking at the mentally ill in a *new* way they made *new* assumptions, and the mentally ill were then treated in a *different* way. The problem in corrections, the underlying assumptions have never changed, and if those assumptions are wrong, then naturally every structure built upon them is sure to fall.

The criminal as a "bad" person probably does exist, but our prisons are also filled with other criminals who, even if they do know the difference between right and wrong, may still be incapable of behavioral control. Repetitive sexual criminals, for example, though not "insane" by either legal or psychiatric definition, are often men who are driven and tormented by cravings which they know are morally reprehensible, and often they are filled with guilt and disgust for themselves. But imprisonment and punishment doesn't always deter them. They may be in the grip of forces they can't control.

Then we have criminals from the so-called deprived cultures. Raised in poverty, surrounded by vice and crime, they are taught values different from the values of the wider culture, and what is criminal for us is almost the norm for them. The way the greater culture defines right and wrong is not the way *their* culture defines right and wrong. This kind of criminal can understand and accept when he is punished for stealing; he is less likely to feel he has been "bad" when he seeks revenge for a wrong, when he smokes or peddles dope, when he fathers illegitimate children, or when he cheats on the welfare system. He comes from a culture which values today because tomorrow isn't promised, where he is taught that if you don't beat the system the system will surely beat you. We cannot divorce the actual criminal act from the whole psychosocial atmosphere. But if indeed we are dealing with a "bad" person whose "badness" must be cured, then we place him in the morally impoverished environment of the prison which tends to duplicate the environment he came from, and then expect that he will somehow learn "better" survival skills. Absurdity upon absurdity, and then we wonder why the recidivism rate won't go away.

Finally, we have the chronic criminals for whom there is no readymade explanation, criminals who fail consistently at their criminal occupation, incompetent criminals, the antisocial personalities, yesterday's psychopaths and sociopaths, who tomorrow may wear yet another label. Their criminal behavior may have little to do with familial or cultural influences. On the surface, at any rate, they don't seem to be emotionally distressed, but their will to fail dominates their lives. They are drawn to penitentiaries as moths to a flame, and if punishment must be a consequence of failure, then punishment must be accepted. It's not punishment they're seeking, and moral right and wrong has little to do with their behavior; the goal is to avoid the intolerable ambiguity of freedom.

Let's assume that there are criminals who are simply "bad," the immoral dregs of our society, and I believe there are criminals like this on whom we should waste little sympathy. I don't know that I could spot one just by looking, but I have examined men in whom I could find no redeeming feature and who I believe should be kept locked up for as long as the law will allow. Shouldn't every criminal at least have the opportunity to change? For even the criminal who perhaps least merits our care and concern will probably return to society someday, and our own self-interest, if not our humanism, demands that we protect ourselves. We don't do that; we don't meet our obligations to ourselves and to our society when we simply send men to prison and do nothing more.

One thing stands out: if we do no more than punish, if we simply imprison for some magic number of years, we can expect a recidivism rate of 65% or more; but if we treat, we can reduce that rate. Admittedly, that rate isn't always reduced sufficiently to justify the time and the expense, but perhaps there are intangible benefits. If we communicate to the prisoner that he is worthless and incapable of change, this merely reinforces his view of himself, and behaviorally he will attempt to meet both our expectations and his own. But if we suggest that change is possible, if we communicate to the prisoner that he can be something more than the sum of his sins, then maybe he will begin to believe and to take the first steps, however hesitant, to peace with himself and with his fellow man.

REFERENCES

Abel, G. G., Becker, J. V., & Cunningham-Rathner, J. (1984). Complications, consent, and cognition in sex between children and adults. *International Journal of Law and Psychiatry, 7,* 89–103.

Abel, G. G., & Blanchard, E. B. (1976). The measurement and generation of sexual arousal in male sexual deviates. In M. Herson, R. M. Eisler, & P. M. Miller (Eds.), *Progress in behavior modification, Vol. 2* (pp. 99–136). New York: Academic Press.

Abel, G. G., Mittleman, M. S., & Becker, J. V. (1983). *Sexual offenders: Results of assessment and recommendations for treatment.* Paper presented to the World Congress of Behavior Therapy.

Adler, G. (1986). Psychotherapy of the narcissistic personality disordered patient: Two contrasting approaches. *American Journal of Psychiatry, 143,* 430–436.

Adler, G., & Shapiro, L. N. (1973). Some difficulties in the treatment of aggressive acting-out patients. *American Journal of Psychotherapy, 27,* 548–556.

Aldrich, C. K. (1987). Acting out and acting up: The superego lacuna revisited. *American Journal of Orthopsychiatry, 57,* 402–406.

American Psychiatric Association (1952). *Diagnostic and statistical manual: Mental disorders.* Washington, DC: Author.

American Psychiatric Association (1968). *Diagnostic and statistical manual of mental disorders* (2nd ed.). Washington, DC: Author.

American Psychiatric Association (1980). *Diagnostic and statistical manual of mental disorders* (3rd ed.). Washington, DC: Author.

American Psychiatric Association (1987). *Diagnostic and statistical manual of mental disorders* (3rd ed., revised). Washington, DC: Author.

Anderson, G. S., & Nutter, R. W. (1975). Clients and outcomes of a methadone treatment program. *International Journal of the Addictions, 10,* 937–948.

Araji, S., & Finkelhor, D. (1985). Explanations of pedophilia: Review of empirical research. *Bulletin of the American Academy of Psychiatry and the Law, 13,* 17–37.

Arnold, W. R., & Stiles, B. (1972). A summary of increasing use of "group methods" in correctional institutions. *International Journal of Group Psychotherapy, 22,* 77–92.

Ausubel, D. P. (1961). Causes and types of narcotic addiction: A psychosocial view. *Psychiatric Quarterly, 35,* 523–531.

Bach-y-Rita, G., & Veno, A. (1974). Habitual violence: A profile of 62 men. *American Journal of Psychiatry, 131,* 1015–1017.

Bale, R. N. (1979). Outcome research in therapeutic communities for drug abusers: A critical review 1963–1975. *International Journal of the Addictions, 14,* 1053–1074.

Barley, W. D. (1986). Behavioral and cognitive treatment of criminal and delinquent behavior. In W. R. Reid, D. Dorr, J. I. Walker, & J. W. Bonner (Eds.), *Unmasking the psychopath* (pp. 159–190). New York: Norton.

Barton, M. A. (1980). Drug histories and criminality: Survey of the inmates of State correctional facilities, January 1974. *International Journal of the Addictions, 15,* 233–258.

Bejerot, N. (1972). A theory of addiction as an artificially induced drive. *American Journal of Psychiatry, 128,* 842–846.

Bender, L., & Blau, A. (1937). The reactions of children to sexual relations with adults. *American Journal of Orthopsychiatry, 7,* 500–518.

Berlin, F. S. (1983). Sex offenders: A biomedical perspective and a status report on biomedical treatment. In J. G. Greer & I. R. Stuart (Eds.), *The sexual aggressor* (pp. 83–123). New York: Van Nostrand Rheinhold.

Berlin, F. S. (1985). Pedophilia. *Medical Aspects of Human Sexuality, 19* (8), 79, 82–85, 88.

Berlin, F. S., & Coyle, G. S. (1981). Sexual deviation syndromes. *The Johns Hopkins Medical Journal, 149,* 119–125.

Berlin, F. S., & Krout, E. (1986). Pedophilia: Diagnostic concepts, treatment, and ethical considerations. *American Journal of Forensic Psychiatry, 7,* (1) 13–30.

Berlin, F. S., & Meinecke, C. F. (1981). Treatment of sex offenders with antiandrogenic medication: Conceptualization, review of treatment modalities, and preliminary findings. *American Journal of Psychiatry, 138,* 601–607.

Bettelheim, B. (1967). *The empty fortress.* New York: The Free Press.

Blackmore, J., & Welsh, J. (1983). Selective incapacitation: Sentencing according to risk. *Crime and Delinquency, 29,* 504–528.

Blatt, S. J., McDonald, C., Sugarman, A., & Wilber, C. (1984). Psychodyamic theories of opiate addiction: New directions for research. *Clinical Psychology Review, 4,* 159–189.

Bolton, N., Smith, F. V., Heskin, K. J., & Banister, P. A. (1976). Psychological correlates of long-term imprisonment. *British Journal of Criminology, 16,* 38–47.

Bordenkircher, D. (1974). Prisons and the revolutionary. In American Correctional Association, *Proceedings of the One Hundred and Fourth Annual Congress of Correction of the American Correctional Association* (pp. 102–135). College Park, MD: American Correctional Association.

Boslow, H. M., & Kohlmeyer, W. A. (1963). The Maryland defective delinquency law: An eight year follow-up. *American Journal of Psychiatry, 120,* 118–124.

Boslow, H. M., Rosenthal, D., & Gliedman, L. H. (1958). The Maryland defective delinquency law: Psychiatric implications for treatment of antisocial disorders under the law. *British Journal of Delinquency, 10*, 5–13.

Boslow, H. M., Rosenthal, D., Kandel, A., & Manne, S. (1961). Methods and experiences in group psychotherapy of defective delinquents. *Journal of Social Therapy, 7*, 3–15.

Brandsma, J. M., & Pattison, E. M. (1985). The outcome of group psychotherapy alcoholics: An empirical review. *American Journal of Drug and Alcohol Abuse, 11*, 151–162.

Brody S. A. (1974). The political prisoner syndrome. *Crime and Delinquency, 20*, 97–106.

Brongersma, E. (1984). Aggression against pedophiles. *International Journal of Law and Psychiatry, 7*, 79–87.

Browne, A., & Finkelhor, D. (1986). Impact of child sexual abuse: A review of the research. *Psychological Bulletin, 99*, 66–77.

Bureau of Justice Statistics (1983a). *Prisoners and alcohol* [Bulletin No. NCJ-86223]. Washington, DC: Author.

Bureau of Justice Statistics (1983b). *Prisoners and drugs* [Bulletin No. NCJ-87575]. Washington, DC: Author.

Bureau of Justice Statistics (1984). *Tracking offenders: The child victim* [Bulletin No. NCJ-95785]. Washington, DC: Author.

Bureau of Justice Statistics (1985). *Jail inmates 1983* [Bulletin No. NCJ-99175]. Washington, DC: Author.

Bureau of Justice Statistics (1986). *Population density in state prisons* [Bulletin No. NCJ-103204]. Washington, DC: Author.

Bureau of Justice Statistics (1987a). *Prisoners in 1986* [Bulletin No. NCJ-104864]. Washington, DC: Author

Bureau of Justice Statistics (1987b). *Recidivism of young parolees* [Bulletin No. NCJ-104916]. Washington, DC: Author.

Bursten, B. (1973). *The manipulator.* New Haven: Yale University Press.

Calkins, K. (1970). Time: Perspectives, marking, and styles of usage. *Social Problems, 17*, 487–501.

Carnes, P. (1983). *The sexual addiction.* Minneapolis: Compcare.

Carney, F. J. (1971). Evaluation of psychotherapy in a maximum security prison. *Seminars in Psychiatry, 3*, 363–375.

Carney, F. L. (1972). Some recurring therapeutic issues in group psychotherapy with criminal patients. *American Journal of Psychotherapy, 26*, 34–41.

Carney, F. L. (1973). Three important factors in psychotherapy with criminal patients. *American Journal of Psychotherapy, 27*, 220–231.

Carney, F. L. (1974). The indeterminate sentence at Patuxent. *Crime and Delinquency, 20*, 135–143.

Carney, F. L. (1976). Treatment of the aggressive patient. In D. J. Madden & J. R. Lion (Eds.), *Rage, hate, assault, and other forms of violence* (pp. 223–248). New York: Spectrum.

Carney, F. L. (1977). Outpatient treatment of the aggressive offender. *American Journal of Psychotherapy, 37*, 265–274.

Carney, F. L. (1978). Inpatient treatment programs. In W. H. Reid (Ed.), *The psychopath* (pp. 261–285). New York: Brunner/Mazel.

Carroll, J. F. X. (1980). Similarities and differences of personality and psychopathology between alcoholics and addicts. *American Journal of Drug and Alcohol Abuse, 7*, 219–236.

Chessick, R. D. (1960). The pharmacogenic orgasm in the drug addict. *Archives of General Psychiatry, 3*, 543–555.

Clark, R. (1970). *Crime in America.* New York: Simon and Schuster.

Clear, T. R., & Barry, D. M. (1983). Some conceptual issues in incapacitating offenders. *Crime and Delinquency, 29*, 529–545.

Cleckley, H. (1959). Psychopathic states. In S. Arieti (Ed.), *American handbook of psychiatry:* Vol. 1. (pp. 567–588). New York: Basic Books.

Cleckley, H (1964). *The mask of sanity* (4th ed.). St. Louis: Mosby.

Cohen, A. (1982). The "urge to classify" the narcotic addict: A review of psychiatric classifications. *International Journal of the Addictions, 17*, 213–225.

Cohen, A. (1986). A psychosocial typology of drug addicts and implications for treatment. *International Journal of the Addictions, 21*, 147–154.

Coid, J. (1984). How many psychiatric patients in prison? *British Journal of Psychiatry, 145*, 78–86.

Collins, J. J. (1981). *Drinking and crime.* New York: Guilford Press.

Conn, J. H. (1955). Treatment of symptomatic psychopathy. *Archives of Criminal Psychodynamics, 1*, 111–136.

Connelly, S. (1981, May 11). Whatever happened to little girlhood? *New York Daily News*, pp. 9C–11C.

Constantine, L. L. (1981). The effects of early sexual experiences: A review and synthesis of research. In L. L. Constantine & F. M. Martinson (Eds.), *Children and sex* (pp. 217–244). Boston: Little, Brown.

Contract Research Corporation (1977). *The evaluation of Patuxent Institution: Final report.* Baltimore: Department of Public Safety and Correctional Services.

Cooper, A. J. (1986). Progesterones in the treatment of male sex offenders. *Canadian Journal of Psychiatry, 31*, 73–79.

Cox, M. (1976). Group psychotherapy in a secure setting. *Proceedings of the Royal Society of Medicine, 69*, 215–220.

Cox, V. C., Paulus, P. B., & McCain, G. (1984). Prison crowding research. *American Psychologist, 39*, 1148–1160.

Craig, R. J. (1979). Personality characteristics of heroin addicts: A review of the empirical literature with critique—Part II. *International Journal of the Addictions, 14*, 607–627.

Craig, R. J., Verinis, J. S., & Wexler, S. (1985). Personality characteristics of drug addicts and alcoholics on the Millon Clinical Mutiaxial Inventory. *Journal of Personality Assessment, 49*, 156–160.

Critchlow, B. (1986). The powers of John Barleycorn: Beliefs about the effects of alcohol on social behavior. *American Psychologist, 41,* 751–764.

Dahl. A. A. (1985). Diagnosis of the borderline disorders. *Psychopathology, 18,* 18–28.

Davis, G. C., & Hagop, S. A. (1986). Descriptive, biological, and theoretical aspects of borderline personality disorder. *Hospital and Community Psychiatry, 37,* 685–692.

Davis, R. W. (1985). Assessing offenders: Dying for reprieve. *Journal of Personality Assessment, 49,* 605–612.

Deitch, D. A., & Zweben, J. E. (1984). Coercion in the therapeutic community. *Journal of Psychoactive Drugs, 16,* 35–41.

DeLeon, G. (1984). *The therapeutic community: Study of effectiveness.* Rockville, MD: National Institute on Drug Abuse.

Deutsch, H. (1942). Some forms of emotional disturbance and their relationship to schizophrenia. *Psychoanalytic Quarterly, 11,* 301–321.

Ditkoff, M. (1978, April). Child pornography. *American Humane,* pp. 29–32.

Dixon, K. N., Arnold, L. E., & Calestro, K. (1978). Father-son incest: Underreported psychiatric problem. *American Journal of Psychiatry, 137,* 835–838.

Dupont, R. L. (1972). Heroin addiction treatment and crime reduction. *American Journal of Psychiatry, 128,* 856–860.

Earls, C. M., & Marshall, W. L. (1983). The current state of technology in the laboratory assessment of sexual arousal patterns. In J. G. Greer & I. R. Stuart (Eds.), *The sexual aggressor: Current perspectives on treatment* (pp. 336–362). New York: Van Nostrand Reinhold.

Elliott, F. A. (1978). Neurological aspects of antisocial behavior. In W. H. Reid (Ed.), *The psychopath* (pp. 148–189). New York: Brunner/Mazel.

Empey, L. T. (1985). The natural history of a flatulent career. *The Criminologist, 10* (6), 5–9.

Farrell, J. P. (1986). *Voices behind the wall.* New York: Henry Holt.

Federal Bureau of Investigation (1985). *Crime in the United States.* Washington, DC: U.S. Government Printing Office.

Feldman, H. W. (1968). Ideological supports to becoming and remaining a drug addict. *Journal of Health and Social Behavior, 9,* 131–139.

Fenichel, O. (1945). *The psychoanalytic theory of neurosis.* New York: W.W. Norton.

Fink, L., & Martin, J. P. (1973). Psychiatry and the crisis of the prison system. *American Journal of Psychotherapy, 27,* 579–584.

Finkelhor, D. (1987). The sexual abuse of children: Current research reviewed. *Psychiatric Annals, 17,* 233–237, 241.

Finkelhor, D. (1979). What's wrong with sex between adults and children? *American Journal of Orthopsychiatry, 49,* 692–697.

Finkelhor, D., & Browne, A. (1985). The traumatic impact of child sexual abuse. *American Journal of Orthopsychiatry, 55,* 531–541.

Flanagan, T. J. (1980). The pain of long-term imprisonment. *British Journal of Criminology, 20,* 148–156.

Flanagan, T. J. (1981). Dealing with long-term confinement: Adaptive strategies and perspectives among long-term prisoners. *Criminal Justice and Behavior, 8*, 201–222.

Foucault, M. (1977). *Discipline and punish.* New York: Pantheon Books.

Fowler, R. C., Liskow, B. I., & Tanna, V. L. (1980) Alcoholism, depression, and life events. *Journal of Affective Disorders, 2*, 127–135.

Gallahorn, G. E. (1981). Borderline personality disorders. In J. R. Lion (Ed.), *Personality disorders: Diagnosis and management* (2nd ed., pp. 74–84). Baltimore: Williams and Wilkens.

Gardner, C. S. & Waagner S. (1986). Clinical diagnosis of the as-if personality disorder. *Bulletin of the Menninger Clinic, 50*, 135–147.

Gelinas, D. J. (1983). The persisting negative effects of incest. *Psychiatry, 46*, 312–332.

Gerber, R. J., & McAnany, P. D. (1977). Punishment as refelected in prevailing ideologies. In L. Radzinowicz & M. E. Wolfgang (Eds.), *Crime and justice: Vol. 2. The criminal in the arms of the law* (pp. 54–85). New York: Basic Books.

Gilbert, J. G., & Lombardi, D. N. (1967). Personality characteristics of young male addicts. *Journal of Consulting Psychology, 31*, 536–538.

Greenfeld, L. A. (1985). *Examining recidivism* [Bureau of Justice Statistics Special Report No. NCJ-96501]. Washington, DC: U.S. Department of Justice.

Groth, A. N. (1979). Sexual trauma in the life histories of rapists and child molesters. *Victimology: An International Journal, 4*, 10–16.

Groth, A. N. (1983). Treatment of the sexual offender in a correctional institution. In J. Greer & I. Stuart (Eds.). *The sexual aggressor: Current perspectives on treatment* (pp. 160–176). New York: Van Nostrand Reinhold.

Groth, A. N. (1985, August). *The psychology of sexual offenders against children.* Paper presented at the 93rd Convention of the American Psychological Association, Los Angeles, CA.

Groth, A. N., & Birnbaum, H. J. (1978). Adult sexual orientation and attraction to underage persons. *Archives of Sexual Behavior, 7*, 175–181.

Groth, A. N., & Burgess, A. W. (1977). Motivational intent in the sexual assault of children. *Criminal Justice and Behavior, 4*, 253–264.

Groth, A. N., Burgess, A. W., Birnbaum, H. J., & Gary, T. S. (1978). A study of child molesters: Myths and realities. *LEA Journal of the American Justice Association, 41*, 17–22.

Groth, A. N., Hobson, W. F., & Gary, T. S. (1982). The child molester: Clinical observations. In J. Conte & D. Shore (Eds.), *Social work and child sexual abuse* (pp. 129–144). New York: Hayworth Press.

Groth, A. N., Longo, R. E., & McFadin, J. B. (1982). Undetected recidivism among rapists and child molesters. *Crime and Delinquency, 28*, 450–458.

Grunfeld, B., & Noreik, K. (1986). Recidivism among sex offenders: A follow-up study of 541 Norwegian sex offenders. *International Journal of Law and Psychiatry, 9*, 95–102.

Grupp, S. E. (1971). *Theories of punishment.* Bloomington, IN: Indiana University Press.

Guy, E., Platt, J. J., & Zwerling, I. (1985). Mental health studies of prisoners in an urban jail. *Criminal Justice and Behavior, 12,* 29–35.

Guze, S. B. (1976). *Criminality and psychiatric disorders.* New York: Oxford University Press.

Halleck, S. (1971a). *The politics of therapy.* New York: Science House.

Halleck, S. (1971b). Psychiatry and correctional justice. *Bulletin of the Menninger Clinic, 35,* 402–407.

Hammer, E. F., & Glueck, B. C. (1957). Psychodynamic patterns in sex offenders: A four-factor theory. *Psychiatric Quarterly, 31,* 325–345.

Hare, R. D. (1983). Diagnosis of antisocial personality disorder in two prison populations. *American Journal of Psychiatry, 140,* 887–890.

Hare, R. D. (1985). Comparison of procedures for the assessment of psychopathy. *Journal of Consulting and Clinical Psychology, 53,* 7–16.

Hare, R. D., & Cox, D. N. (1978). Psychophysiological research on psychopathy. In W. H. Reid (Ed.), *The psychopath* (pp. 209–222). New York: Brunner/Mazel.

Hare, R. D., & McPherson, L. M. (1984). Violent and aggressive behavior by criminal psychopaths. *International Journal of Law and Psychiatry, 7,* 35–50.

Harris, J. (1986). *Stranger in two worlds.* New York: Macmillan.

Hesselbrock, M. N., Meyer, R. E., & Keener, J. J. (1985). Psychopathology in hospitalized alcoholics. *Archives of General Psychiatry, 42,* 1050–1055.

Hesselbrock, V. M., Hesselbrock, M. N., & Workman-Daniels (1986). Effect of major depression and antisocial personality on alcoholism: Course and motivational patterns. *Journal of Studies on Alcohol, 47,* 207–212.

Hodges, E. F. (1971). Crime prevention by the indeterminate sentence law. *American Journal of Psychiatry, 128,* 291–295.

Horwitz, L. (1985). Divergent views on the treatment of borderline patients. *Bulletin of the Menninger Clinic, 49,* 525–545.

Ibrahim, A. I. (1974). Deviant sexual behavior in men's prisons. *Crime and Delinquency, 20,* 38–44.

Ingram, M. (1981). Participating victims: A study of sexual offenses with boys. In L. L. Constantine & F. M. Martinson (Eds.), *Children and sex* (pp. 177–187). Boston: Little, Brown.

Jew, C. C., Clanon, T. L., & Mattocks, A. L. (1972). The effectiveness of group psychotherapy in a correctional institution. *American Journal of Psychiatry, 129,* 602–605.

Johnston, J. M. (1972). Punishment of human behavior. *American Psychologist, 27,* 1033–1054.

Kamin, L. J. (1986, April). Is crime in the genes? [Review of *Crime and human nature*]. *Scientific American,* pp. 22–25.

Karpman, B. (1941). On the need for separating psychopathy into two distinct types: The symptomatic and the idiopathic. *Journal of Criminal Psychopathology, 3,* 112–137.

Karpman, B. (1948). Myth of psychopathic personality. *American Journal of Psychiatry, 104,* 523–534.

Karpman, B. (1954). *The sexual offender and his offenses.* New York: Julian Press.

Kaufman, E. (1972). A psychiatrist views an addict self-help program. *American Journal of Psychiatry, 128,* 846–851.

Kennedy, D. B. (1984). A theory of suicide while in police custody. *Journal of Police Science and Administration, 12,* 191–200.

Kernberg, O. (1975). *Borderline conditions and pathological narcissism.* New York: Jason Aronson.

Khantzian, E. J., & Treece, C. (1985). DSM-III psychiatric diagnosis of narcotic addicts. *Archives of General Psychiatry, 42,* 1067–1071.

Kohut, H. (1977). *The restoration of the self.* New York: International Universities Press.

Kozol, H. L. (1959). The psychopath before the law. *New England Journal of Medicine, 260,* 637–644.

Knopp, F. H. (1984). *Retraining adult sexual offenders: Methods and models.* Syracuse, NY: Safer Society Press.

Knopp, F. H., Rosenberg, J., & Stevenson, W. (1986). *Directory of juvenile and adult sex offender treatment programs in the United States.* Syracuse, NY: Safer Society Press.

Langevin, R. (1983). *Sexual strands.* Hillsdale, NJ: Lawrence Erlbaum.

Laws, D. R. (1987). *Prevention of relapse in sex offenders.* Tampa, FL: Florida Mental Health Institute.

Laws, D. R., & Osborn, C. A. (1983). How to build and operate a behavioral laboratory to evaluate and treat sexual deviance. In J. G. Greer & I. R. Stuart (Eds), *The sexual aggressor: Current perspectives on treatment* (pp. 293–335). New York: Van Nostrand Reinhold.

Lejins, P. (1977). The Patuxent experience. *Bulletin of the American Academy of Psychiatry and the Law, 5,* 116–133.

Levine, D. G., Levin, D. B., Sloan, I. H., & Chappel, J. N. (1972). Personality correlates of success in a methadone maintenance program. *American Journal of Psychiatry, 129,* 456–460.

Lewis, A. (1967). *Inquiries in psychiatry.* New York: Science House.

Lewis, C. E. (1984). Alcoholism, antisocial personality, narcotic addiction: An integrative approach. *Psychiatric Developments, 3,* 223–235.

Lewis, C. E., Rice, J., Andeasen, N., Clayton, P., & Endicott, J. (1985). Alcoholism in antisocial and nonantisocial men with unipolar major depression. *Journal of Affective Disorders, 9,* 253–263.

Lindesmith, A. R. (1968). *Addiction and opiates.* Chicago: Aldine.

Lindner, R. M. (1944). *Rebel without a cause.* New York: Grune and Stratton.

Lion, J. R., & Pasternak, S. E. (1975). Countertransference reactions to violent patients. *American Journal of Psychiatry, 130,* 207–210.

Longo, R. E., & Groth, A. N. (1983). Juvenile sexual offenses in the histories of adult rapists and child molesters. *International Journal of Offender Therapy and Comparative Criminology, 27*, 150–155.

McCaghy, C. H. (1968). Drinking and deviance disavowal: the case of child molesters. *Social Problems, 16*, 43–49.

McGrath, R. J., & Carey, C. H. (1987). Treatment of men who molest children: A program description. *Journal of Offender Counseling, 19*, 23–33.

Maddux, J. F., & Bowden, C. L. (1972). Critique of success with methadone mainenance. *American Journal of Psychiatry, 129*, 440–446.

Manne, S. (1967). A communication theory of sociopathic personality. *American Journal of Psychotherapy, 21*, 797–807.

Marks, I. M. (1981). Review of behavioral psychotherapy, II: Sexual disorders. *American Journal of Psychiatry, 138*, 750–756.

Marshall, W. L., & Christie, M. M. (1981). Pedophilia and aggression. *Criminal Justice and Behavior, 8*, 145–158.

Martinson, R. (1977). What works?—A comparative assessment. In L. Radzinowicz & M. E. Wolfgang (Eds.), *Crime and justice: Vol. 3. The criminal under restraint* (pp. 3–32). New York: Basic Books.

Mathias, R. E., & Sinberg, R. (1985). Psychotherapy in correctional settings. *International Journal of Offender Therapy and Comparative Criminology, 29*, 265–275.

Meisenhelder, T. (1985). An essay on time and the phenomenology of imprisonment. *Deviant Behavior, 6*, 39–56.

Menninger, K. (1968). *The crime of punishment.* New York: Viking.

Milgram, S. (1968). Conditions of obedience and disobedience to authority. *International Journal of Psychiatry, 6*, 259–276.

Miller, R. E. (1984). Nationwide profile of female inmate substance involvement. *Journal of Psychoactive Drugs, 16*, 319–326.

Mitford, J. (1973). *Kind and usual punishment.* New York: Knopf.

Monroe, R. R. (1972). *Episodic behavioral disorders.* Cambridge: Harvard University Press.

Myers, T. (1986). An analysis of context and alcohol consumption in a group of criminal events. *Alcohol and Alcoholism, 21*, 389–395.

Nacci, P. L., & Kane, T. R. (1984). Inmate sexual aggression: Some evolving propositions, empirical findings, and mitigating counterforces. *Journal of Offender Counseling, Services and Rehabilitation, 9*, 1–20.

Newmark, J. J. (1979, April 29). Is sex in ads X-rated? *St. Louis Post-Dispatch*, Section G, p. 1.

Nurco, D. N., Ball, J. C., Shaffer, J. W., & Hanlon, T. E. (1985). The criminality of narcotic addicts. *Journal of Nervous and Mental Disease, 173*, 94–102.

Nurco, D. N., Ball, J. C., Shaffer, J. W., Kinlock, T. W., & Langrod, J. L. (1986). A comparison by race/ethnicity of narcotic addict crime rates in Baltimore, New York, and Philadelphia. *American Journal of Drug and Alcohol Abuse, 12*, 297–307.

Nyswander, M. (1959). Drug addictions. In S. Arieti (Ed.), *American handbook of psychiatry:* Vol 1 (pp. 614–622). New York: Basic Books.

O'Brien, C. P., Ehrman, R. N., & Ternes, J. W. (1984). Classical conditioning in opiate dependence. *National Institute on Drug Abuse Research Monograph, 49,* 35–46.

O'Brien, W. B., & Biase, D. V. (1984). The therapeutic community: A current perspective. *Journal of Psychoactive Drugs, 16,* 9–21.

O'Donnell, J. A. (1964). A follow-up of New York narcotic addicts: Morality, relapse, and abstinence. *American Journal of Orthopsychiatry, 34,* 948–954.

Okpaku, S. O. (1986). Psychoanalytically oriented psychotherapy of substance abuse. *Advances in Alcohol and Substance Abuse, 6,* 17–33.

Panton, J. H., & Brisson, R. C. (1971). Characteristics associated with drug abuse in a state prison population. *Corrective Psychiatry and Journal of Social Therapy, 17,* 3–33.

Parker, H., & Parker, S. (1986). Father-daughter sexual abuse. *American Journal of Orthopsychiatry, 56,* 531–549.

Patuxent Instittution (1973). *A progress report.* Jessup, MD: Author.

Patuxent Institution (1984). *Annual report for 1983.* Jessup, MD: Author.

Persons, J. B. (1986). The advantage of studying psychological phenomena rather than psychiatric diagnoses. *American Psychologist, 41,* 1252–1260.

Peyrot, M. (1985). Narcotics Annonymous: Its history, structure and approach. *International Journal of the Addictions, 20,* 1509–1523.

Phillips, J. A. (1981). Narcissistic personality. In J. R. Lion (Ed.), *Personality disorders: Diagnosis and management* (2nd ed., pp. 65–73). Baltimore: Williams and Wilkens.

Phillips, R. (1981, Feb.1). How children become prostitutes. *Chicago Tribune,* Section 12, pp. 1, 4.

Pithers, W. D., & Laws, D. R. (in press). The penile plethysmograph: Uses and abuses in assessment and treatment of sexual aggressors. In B. Schwartz (Ed.), *Sex offenders: Issues in treatment.* Washington, DC: National Institute of Corrections.

Pithers, W. D., Marques, J. K., Gibat, C. C., & Marlatt, G. A. (1983). Relapse prevention with sexual aggressives: A self-control model of treatment and maintenance of change. In J. G. Greer & I. R. Stuart (Eds.), *The sexual aggressor: Current perspectives on treatment* (pp. 214–239). New York: Van Nostrand Reinhold.

Porchke, W. R. (1970). The addiction cycle: A learning theory-peer group model. *Corrective Psychiatry and Journal of Social Therapy, 16,* 74–81.

Powell, R. W. (1973). Punishment reconsidered. In J. G. Cull & R. E. Hardy (Eds.), *Law enforcement and correctional rehabilitation* (pp. 92–98). Springfield, IL: Charles C. Thomas.

Price, J. (1984). Homosexuality in a Victorian male prison. *Mental Health in Australia, 1,* 3–12.

Protter, B., & Travin, S. (1982). Profile of defendants seen for pre-sentence psychiatric examination. *Bulletin of the American Academy of Psychiatry and the Law, 10,* 123–134.

Rado, S. (1933). Psychoanalysis of pharmacothymia. *Psychoanalytic Quarterly,* 2, 1–23.

Rappaport, R. G. (1971). Group therapy in prison. *International Journal of Group Psychotherapy,* 21, 489–492.

Rasch, W. (1981). The effects of indeterminate detention: A study of men sentenced to life imprisonment. *International Journal of Law and Psychiatry,* 4, 417–431.

Reiblich,G. K., & Hubbard, H. H. (1950). *An indeterminate sentence law for defective delinquents* [Research Report No. 291]. Baltimore: Legislative Council of Maryland.

Reid, W. H. (1978). The sadness of the psychopath. In W. H. Reid (Ed.). *The psychopath* (pp. 7–21). New York: Brunner/Mazel.

Reid, W. H. (1981). The antisocial personality and related syndromes. In J. R. Lion (Ed.), *Personality disorders: Diagnosis and Management* (2nd ed., pp. 133–162). Baltimore: Williams and Wilkens.

Reid, W. H. (1985). The antisocial personality: A review. *Hospital and Community Psychiatry,* 36, 831–837.

Richards, B. (1978). The experience of long-term imprisonment. *British Journal of Criminology,* 18, 162–169.

Richardson, D., & Campbell, J. L. (1982). Alcohol and rape: the effect of alcohol on attribution of blame for rape. *Personality and Social Psychology Bulletin,* 8, 468–476.

Rounsaville, B. J., Dolinsky, Z. S., Babor, T. F., & Meyer, R. E. (1987). Psychopathology as a predictor of treatment outcome in alcoholics. *Archives of General Psychiatry,* 44, 505–513.

Samenow, S. E. (1984). *Inside the criminal mind.* New York: Times Books.

Sapsford, R. J. (1978). Life-sentence prisoners: psychological changes during sentence. *British Journal of Criminology,* 18, 128–145.

Sargent, D. A. (1974). Confinement and ego regression: Some consequences of enforced passivity. *International Journal of Psychiatry in Medicine,* 5, 143–151.

Savitt, R. A. (1963). Psychoanalytic study of addiction: Ego structure in narcotic addicts. *Psychoanalytic Quarterly,* 33, 43–57.

Schilder, P. (1953). *Medical psychology.* New York: International Universities Press.

Schuckit, M. A. (1983). Alcoholism and other psychiatric disorders. *Hospital and Community Psychiatry,* 34, 1022–1027.

Schuckit, M. A. (1985). The clinical implication of primary diagnostic groups among alcoholics. *Archives of General Psychiatry,* 42, 1043–1049.

Schwitzgebel, R. K. (1971). Learning theory approaches to the treatment of criminal behavior. *Seminars in Psychiatry,* 3, 328–344.

Seghorn, T. K., Prentky, R. A., & Boucher, M. S. (1987). Childhood sexual abuse in the lives of sexually aggressive offenders. *Journal of the American Academy of Child and Adolescent Psychiatry,* 26, 262–267.

Selby, J. W., Calhoun, L. G., Jones, J. M., & Matthews, L. (1980). Families of incest: A collation of clinical impressions. *International Journal of Social Psychiatry, 26,* 7–16.

Shelly, J. A., & Bassin, A. (1965). A new treatment approach for drug addicts. *Corrective Psychiatry and Journal of Social Therapy, 11,* 186–195.

Showers, J., Farber, E. D., Joseph, J. A., Ohins, L., & Johnson, C. F. (1983). The sexual victimization of boys: A three-year survey. *Health Values, 7* (4), 15–18.

Silfen, P. (1986). Psychotherapy of mentally disturbed criminals: Illusion or reality? *Medicine and Law, 5,* 427–431.

Snyder, S., Pitts, W. M., & Pokorny, A. D. (1985). Affective and behavioral features of DSM-III borderline personality disorder. *Psychopathology, 18,* 3–10.

Sobell, L. C., & Sobell, M. B. (1975). Drunkenness, a "special circumstance" in crimes of violence: Sometimes. *International Journal of the Addictions, 10,* 869–882.

Soothill, K. L., & Gibbens, T. C. N. (1978). Recidivism of sexual offenders: A reappraisal. *British Journal of Criminology, 18,* 267–276.

Spencer, M. J., & Dunkle, P. (1986). Child sexual abuse. *Pediatrics, 78,* 133–138.

Srivastava, S. P. (1974). Sex life in an Indian male prison. *The Indian Journal of Social Work, 35,* 21–33.

Steadman, H. J. (1977). A new look at recidivism among Patuxent inmates. *Bulletin of the American Academy of Psychiatry and the Law, 5,* 200–209.

Sykes, G. M. (1958). *The society of captives: A study of a maximum security prison.* Princeton: Princeton University Press.

Sykes, G. M., & Messinger, S. L. (1977). Inmate social systems. In L. Radzinowicz & M. E. Wolfgang (Eds.), *Crime and justice: Vol. 3. The criminal under restraint* (pp. 185–193). New York: Basic Books.

Teitlebaum, S. H. (1965). The psychopathic style of life and its defensive function. *American Journal of Psychotherapy, 19,* 126–136.

Tingle, D., Barnard, G. W., Robbins, L., Newman, G., & Hutchinson, D. (1986). Childhood and adolescent characteristics of pedophiles and rapists. *International Journal of Law and Psychiatry, 9,* 103–116.

Toch, H. (1975). *Men in crisis.* Chicago: Aldine.

Travin, S., Bluestone, H, Coleman, E., Cullen, K., & Melella, J. (1986). Pedophile types and treatment perspectives. *Journal of Forensic Sciences, 31,* 614–620.

Treece, C., & Khantzian, E. J. (1986). Psychodynamic factors in the development of drug dependence. *Psychiatric Clinics of North America, 9,* 399–412.

Vaillant, G. E. (1966). A twelve year follow-up of New York narcotic addicts: The relation of treatment to outcome. *American Journal of Psychiatry, 122,* 727–737.

Vaillant, G. E. (1975). Sociopathy as a human process. *Archives of General Psychiatry, 32,* 178–183.

Vaillant, G. E., & Milofsky, E. S. (1982). The etiology of alcoholism: A prospective viewpoint. *American Psychologist, 37,* 494–503.

Watkins, J. C. (1964). The modification of the subculture in a corectional institution. In American Correctional Association, *Proceedings of the Ninety-Fourth Congress of Corrections* (pp. 161–171). College Park, MD: American Correctional Association.

Weissman, M. M., Myers, J. K., & Harding, P. S. (1980). Prevelence and psychiatric heterogeneity of alcoholism in a United States urban community. *Journal of Studies on Alcohol, 41,* 672–681.

Weppner, R. S., Stephens, R. C., & Conrad, H. T. (1972). Methadone: Some aspects of its legal and illegal use. *American Journal of Psychiatry, 129,* 451–455.

Werner, H. (1948). *Comparative psychology of mental development.* Chicago: Follett.

Wikler, A. (1965). Conditioning factors in opiate addiction and relapse. In D. I. Wilner & G. G. Kassenbaum (Eds.), *Narcotics* (pp. 85–100). New York: McGraw-Hill.

Wikler, A. (1971). Some implications of conditioning theory for the problem of drug abuse. *Behavioral Science, 17,* 92–97.

Williams, J. S., & Singh, B. K. (1986). Alcohol use and antisocial experiences. *Advances in Alcohol and Substance Abuse, 6,* 65–75.

Wilson, J. Q., & Boland, B. (1977). Incapacitation. In L. Radzinowicz & M. E. Wolfgang (Eds.), *Crime and justice: Vol. 3. The criminal under restraint* (pp. 174–182). New York: Basic Books.

Wilson, J. Q., & Herrnstein, R. J. (1985). *Crime and human nature.* New York: Simon and Schuster.

Wurmser, L. (1984). More respect for the neurotic process: Comments on the problem of narcissism in severe psychopathology, especially the addictions. *Journal of Substance Abuse Treatment, 1,* 37–45.

Yochelson, S., & Samenow, S. E. (1976). *The criminal personality:* Vol. 1. New York: Jason Aronson.

Zilboorg, G. (1954). *The psychology of the criminal act and punishment.* New York: Harcourt, Brace.

Zucker, R. A., & Lisansky Gomberg, E. S. (1986). Etiology of alcoholism reconsidered. *American Psychologist, 41,* 783–793.

Zwerling, I., & Rosenbaum, M. (1959). Alcohol addiction and personality. In S. Arieti (Ed.). *American handbook of psychiatry:* Vol. 1 (pp. 623–644.). New York: Basic Books.